INNOVATIVE TECHS
YOUR LIFE-CHANGER

Leon Dann

INNOVATIVE TECHS
YOUR LIFE-CHANGER

LEON DANN   B.A; M.S Ed

REVISED EDITION

ISBN 978-1-7750441-1-6, Canada

Acknowledgement

To: Vanessa Bucknor, my 4 1/2 years granddaughter, who displays alarming reading skills. Reading at grade 2 reading level. Her voluntary approach of reading shopping lists of items prepared in her grandmother's lower-case handwriting. Just taking a look at family-member text message she reads with ease and smoothness. She demonstrates curious-mind capacity as she searches in a standardized procedure for her favourite, kiddies shows or videos and will verbally identify any known videos or shows as they scrolled by .

In addition, her continued display of recognizing details, her responses, and uses of abstract statements open-up the question; to what extent, digital facilities generated by Digital Technology influence developmental learning in this toddler? Many may suggest that the concept of "genes hereditary has kicked in as her parents are smart parents. So, she inherits the smart genes from her parents that influences her developmental displays. However, I recommend that, as Educators upgrade their education programs, a close look could be made if there is a necessity to incorporate and implement smart genes add-ons to Education Gifted Programs, as Digital Technology embraces the "Smart concept" in numerous areas of our lifestyles.

To: Mathias Leon Daniel Gayle, my 2years and 8 months old grandson who reminds me that basic to digital technology are movements which are the flow of atoms. This is demonstrated in the frequent display of fast movement along the carpeted-floor and the motion of his arms reminds us that basic to Digital Technology is motion.

Basic to the structure of everything are atoms and these atoms are in motion as exemplified in the fast movement of the Internet factored very much as deployed in Digital Technology basic to Digital Technology Era we now enjoy. But as we know that the "eyes" do not reveal everything. The exceptional motions displays are representation of hidden exceptional, abilities inherited from one or two parents that determined to come to bloom in later development.

Introduction

INNOVATIVE TECHS YOUR LIFE-CHANGER

In a vibrant, highly commercialized Western culture that Canada and The United States offer, consumers have fallen in love with products and services linked to this new technology, Digital Technology. Actively used in consumer products, deployed in the commercial and industrial sectors of business and heavily utilized in Social Media they generate interesting conversation pieces and pull in consumers to fill their shopping bags. Stakeholders such as investors and businessmen, scientists are pulled together by the creation of the Digital Ecosystems which offer all the facilities needed to foster the development of variety of digital technologies to create products and services from the initial stage of conception to the final sale of the product or service to the hands of the consumers. While at the same time each stakeholder's personal needs are met. Ranging from personal use of digital product, obtaining a salary higher than the average worker, or etching his name on the famous pages of history.

Conception of an idea, and working through some basic processes has its origin from the individual's personal basement, the office, the laboratory, there they act upon the new idea. From the idea gives rise to new products, and create new services, give value to existing valueless, commodity focussing on digital products and ser-

-vices some of which is in high demand, as products and services are intertwined in the cultural fabric of western lifestyle. While at the same time, innovators stick to the main purpose that drives them to the use of this technology, to maximize their monetary benefits as they sometimes struggle through the various processes. As a result of a variety of efforts of innovators, scientists, technologists, researchers, frontline workers, digital technol-ogy has evolved, creating digital innovations reshaping the technology landscape, creating new products and services. New lifestyles emerged, catering for the human social needs, the discovery, and application of new resources, personal data gives rise to new industries. As the individual moves about the changing, technology landscape he begins to experience a digital make-over.

He is no longer a person of loneliness for he is connected to networks, globally so influenced by international intricacies. Easy access to Social Media platforms connect him with distant friends. Personal access to digital wearables, do not only enhance the emerging, visual image but allows him to pay attention to preferred lifestyles, such as paying attention to his/her keep-fit level. As the individual interacts with smart machine with the capability to think smartly, as humans, he is immersed in the intricacies of smart technology, which offers access to Smart Cars, Smart Homes, and Smart Cities, an existence in smart wrld.

The deployment of digital technology has begun to reshape society, specifically, industry, commerce and consumers' purchasing attitude. The citizenry is awakened to the quiet disruption that Digital Technology generates, they do not have to protect themselves, they embrace the technology for they love this Digital Technology.

For although there are those who use the technology invade their privacy the technology drives much excitement in their lives. The deployment of Digital Technology in industry offers a higher functioning level of efficiency especially in product manufacturing. While the use of data analysis adds another dimension to the commercial profile of the average person in Western society. Recognition that data has its effectiveness in planning, predicting efficiency, and targeting the specialized profile of the individual is enhanced. He supplies labor to the industry, he is a consumer of manufactured products, and he now has personal information, (data) when put together with others, has created a multi-billion dollar industry, demonstrated by Social Media platforms.

Products such as, mobile phone, facial recognition cameras, digital sensors, driverless automobiles, are just few products, that create a niche in the market. While entrepreneurs of digital starts-up industries focusing on Toronto, Montreal Canada and Silicon Valley and Seattle in U.S.A turn out products to satisfy demands of excited consumers, they offer a peek into the digital technology future by presenting samplings of; Smart City, Driverless Cars, Smart Homes, Smart Home Security Systems and Space Vacationing.

Used frequently are portable digital devices along with city and household security services that draw consumer curiosity and ignite attention. As new social lifestyles are created and so taking roots in our daily lives. So, lifestyle has begun to undergo visual change, the change is catchy and compelling as mobile phones are now "a cannot-do-without product". Business forecasters released reliable projection of multi-billion dollar industries facilitated by "The Internet of Things," offering the projection of jobs in great numbers are just a part of the mixture of excitement. With the backdrop of an economy where the unemployment is already at 40 years low for the USA while Canada embraces and enjoys a significant low unemployment up to prior to the pandemic.

There is no doubt Covid-19 has almost pushed the economy of Western society in recession nut business confidence will one more be elevated. As business turn out Digital Technology to reshape the nations and force an individual make-over image. Recipients are pushed to a higher level of comfort and as they bask in new products and services generated by innovative technology.

As individuals embrace digital technology, and utilize the application of the technology in all phases of their life styles, the noticeable rush to deploy the technology in tradition, commercial and industrial and industrial equipment systems, to offer services and functional products for higher level of satisfaction, is welcoming as the citizenry has become a techno-logically smart people. As they embrace the offer to enjoy the comfort and time saving that Smart Homes and Smart cities offer. The accept-ing, reality and new identity that western man is connected globally offers the scope to see himself with new emerging roles far beyond community and national boundaries, to break from the consumer-ma-nipulating puppetry strings, possibly to participate in reshaping the transforming technology landscape with digital technology, possibly to make input to the little pieces that fit together in creating a new development model to underdeveloped, global communities. To har-ness the emerging technology to create new personal commodities that offer personal, individual value in society as personal data has started to do. So, enabling the creation of a new developmental model in contrast to the model left behind as result of historical Discovery and Exploration Era.

That new digital development model seeks reject the current practice business objective, "profit maximization" for "profit distribu-tion" so offering a greater share of the profit pie of their employment, especially workers of the middle and lower levels.

The recognition that digital equipment and devices produce great abundance of data, offers the recognition of data as a commodity, so having significant monetary value. This is the era where high speed computer systems, along with the high-speed internet using digital technology delivers data, shaping consumers products and services, as well as consumers purchasing attitude globally. High speed Internet facilitates an inter-connected world at a cheap cost so catching the attention of the entrepreneurs, the innovators, and consumers.

As businessmen, innovators and other enthusiasts are pulled together by the Digital Exchange Theory. It is the "Accommodation principle" of The Digital Exchange Theory that offers participants of various business activities, the opportunities to maximize their financial benefits as they involved in these activities required to produce digital products and services. As a result, new industries spring up, new business models spring up creating wealth. Employment soars, so shoppers have more expendable funds to spend on themselves, the Social Media Platforms create access points for required needs.

We see Social Media platforms have become the new formats to offer comfort to leisure frolickers. As the hands of history have become active, prints of history and the hands of carvings are not only of the obvious, but attention is drawn to what many of Western culture yawns for to be "filthy rich" digital technology has cast and created the richest man in the world, while history has acknowledged, carved the name and image of Elon Musk of Tesla and Jeff Bezos, Amazon CEO, among the richest men in the world.

As products and services for industry and consumers are churned out, attention is focussed on the mobile phone. This product has become "a cannot-do-without". It's not only made impression on the minds of many but etches in history that the mobile phone is the first device being used to supply so many services. This device wakes-up the user in the morning and being the last device used before going to bed at nights.

With upcoming of the 5G Technology which significantly impacts the mobile phone giving it high-definition quality and speed likely to be 100 times faster than speed now used by the mobile phone.

The changing technology landscape has been a glitter of hope, showing the pathway to those who itch for the job security as never seen before, as IOT generate products and services that enable users to function more efficiently. In Canada and the USA in 2018, thousands of new jobs have been created, employment is in a record high. Digital technology gives rise to the experimenting of Smart City where those who sit in the seats of driverless automobile can pinch themselves to justify that the act is real, not a dream.

Some may not readily embrace the concept of an automobile having the capability to drive people about the city without a human manually steering it. But soon may recognize there is no need for a driver for digital, artificial intelligent technology is the brain of the automobile that moves about the city safely. For as it moves about the city pulling data from sensors along the roadside, as it is needed to make its next technical, serious move.

Systems such as Education, Water, Security, Transport, Health to name a few, are important. So it is logical that these established systems that offer a variety of services when they are driven by artificial intelligence technology, these services are likely to be more efficient. Like identifying problems within the specific areas of the services, and so fix them before they break down. In addition, residents are likely to increase their participation level within the city. Household equipment such as water heater, just one of the future, "***Internet of Things***", of a consumer may send a reliable message to the City Hall, suggesting that there is potential clogging of the drainage systems along the street in that specific neighborhood. If acted on quickly, such data could be used to prevention disruption within the city water services.

It is evident that The application of Artificial Intelligence technol-ogy in systems that facilitate city services do appeal to city managers and mayors. As city residents embrace the emerging Smart Homes, such response is merely a continuation of digital, cultural transforma-tion that is inevitably demanding a response from residents, it impacts. We must remember that residents usually have the feeling that they are the king/or queen of their individual homes. Household appliances, are hooked up hooked up to the *Internet* and having the capability to pick-up data, make data and send it to manufacturers, other devices as well as other appliances. During the process these devices and appli-ances have the capabilities to picking up data within its environments, so there goes another component of personal privacy.

As Artificial Intelligent machine picks-up and transfers data over the Internet, residents' data could also be picked up and being transferred to unwanted destinations. So, the home a place usually a place of privacy may become a place where the resident has to be look-ing over his/her shoulder. But at present, residents seem to demon-strate welcoming gestures to artificial intelligence operated appliances and devices right in their place of residence. There is a downside to the use of Big Data.

Since it is a known fact that Big Data never dies but seems to disappear to prevent personal data to be in the hands of unscrupulous individuals, is essential. So, I have identified the Domain of Dormancy of data which I have named, ***Disappearing Horizon of Information. This is*** where personal data stays dormant, it is a risky area as your personal data, possibly can be access and can be used against you. It can be resurrected and used against the individual as seen where a prominent superstar, personal data has been resurrected, used against him sending him to prison even at his old age. The possibility to create apps to alert users so putting them on guard as to where they are at in terms of their safety of personal data is a possible solution.

As these devices are hooked up to the Internet, users can be away in distant places as far as the Caribbean or Europe on vacation, using the mobile phone or computer can monitor the security cameras installed to cover the inside and or outside of the house. In the same note, when residents about to leave work, he /she may adjust the ther-mostat at home so that upon entering home there is a warm home to come to. The kettle or the coffee pot can be turned on, so having avail-able, upon entry at home, a cup of hot coffee. Since machines in our homes, talk to one another, on the way home from work the resident can communicate with the stove to take an inventory of food stuff and relay the information back to that resident so that he/she may replace the needed grocery, by shopping on way towards home that's the pro-jection of some innovators.

At home a digital, sensor, a part of the security system is on the alert, as the security camera picks up someone moving towards the home, the camera which has face recognition capability, analyses the face, and so deems him an intruder. The camera, then communicates to other sensors attached over the house, alerting them that there is an intruder at the house so generating an alertness from the sensors of the security system, so relaying information to the mobile phone or computer which ever device being used. In this way the resident is alert and so may utilize his/her options. So, Generation Zoomers, no doubt welcome the application of digital technology in these numerous areas but also extend a hand to those who are timely coming on board.

As new, home appliances, as well as machinery used in areas of industry, even consumers' devices and consumers' wearables are built, they are attached with digital technology. There still exists all forms of industrial equipment as well as numerous plug-ins impacting many areas in our lives. As their replacement are built, they are designed to be controlled by the new Digital Technology systems. As electrical circuits were used during the Industrial Revolution to run all equipment and machinery with moving parts, similarly, all equipment and machinery will be attached with digital circuitry. In effect, there will be so many devices, machinery, equipment, sensors, artificial intelligent machine attached to The Internet, that innovators come up with the term, "Internet of Things".

It is predicted The Internet of Things industry will generate a multi-billion U.S.D industry, globally. But as the Internet of Things, predict the great possibility that lies a head for all plug-ins, that is, all things with moving parts and electrical circuits, so innovators have come up with a business model, that is portable and when applied will generate digital products and services, this is the Digital Ecosystems. This concept is borrowed from the discipline of biology where Ecosystems suggest, a place where living things thrive, cooperatively and utilize supportive resources, usually existing in harmony with one another.

Innovators have figured out all the necessary, supportive, resources needed to spring-up digital products and services not only in Canada and USA but also has application globally which also includes a commercial and consumer market necessary to purchase these products and services.

The portability of this models offers hope for global, deployment, even in remote countries that have basic infrastructure inclusive of high speed internet and electrical energy. Since Digital Technology Era is a period where existing Digital Technology allows room for improvement, creeping up on consumers the anticipated technology focussing on mobile phone called the 5G technology, suggesting that the best is yet to come to enhance the quality of the mobile phone.

It is anticipated that the 5G technology carries data 100 times faster than the present speed while the video quality is comparable to high definition television the drawback that faces the West is that because the technology has its origin in Asia, it may consist of technology that puts the security of both countries at risk. Since Canada and USA will not stand for nothing but the best, their scientists, engineers, technologists, and innovators will come up with solutions to raise the quality of mobile phone to be among the best in the world.

The deployment of Digital technology is a silent Industrial Revolution positioned in changing the technology landscapes of Industry. This technology is positioned to impact commerce, lifestyles and reshaping consumers purchasing attitude as they undergo a digital make over within our Western culture with the capability to impact global communities. As players with power, to enforce change, and existence of the application of portable ecosystems which carry all the components necessary to accommodate the production of digital services and products from the start to placement in the hands of consumers, we just could see the deployment of a new developmental model, will taking shape. Of course, many form of models now in use begin their shape during the historical period of Exploration and Conquest whose model of development leaves many communities underdeveloped to this day.

As digital innovative technology impacts industry, consumers' products and lifestyles of Western people, individuals have taken on a digital image. Most household has at least a laptop computer, a desk top computer or a tablet while each individual mobile phone hooked up to at least 6 services attached to the internet. Individuals communicate digitally, meaning they send information by email, texting, Social Media, posting or tweets.

A lap top computer in a carrying case hanging from the shoulder of a user, an earphone plugs into an ear while the user walking along a busy sidewalk peeks at his/her keep fit health monitor attached to his arm for it informs him that he should walk for half an hour that day. He reaches for his mobile phone and quickly sends a text message home. Well this character is more like a character to be deployed in a documentary about Digital Innovation. But realistically, individuals of our major cities have the capabilities to use at least 4 services or devices daily.

This world can be different if the citizenry and moral onlookers, participate with honest conscience to be a part of the mixture of influence. For when the option of "take it or leave it "is not a welcome option but a sentence of delayed, death to live in poverty, then hope rests in the mindset of the power brokers. As the technology brings to Western citizenry that newness, and as they embrace, make- over of culture, lifestyle, new ways of socializing, growing level of wealth, and the mingling of personal moments in happiness. There are others in distant communities where the reality is hanging on to fragile strings of survival, their wishes are just to enjoy a new comfortable level of lifestyle, of basic needs. As Digital Innovations deliver a welcoming, level comfort to some, there are others globally who yearns for their comfort level to be just basic Survival Needs. Digital Innovation can deliver both.

Contents

INNOVATIVE TECHS YOUR LIFE-CHANGER

LEON DANN   B.A; M.S; ED

USA

ISBN 978-1-7750441-1-6, Canada

Innovation Techs Transforming
the Digital Landscape

FIGURE 1-1 The computer is fundamental in the production of goods and services in our innovative industries. Shutterstock infographics.

We love the devices and services that Digital Technology (commonly called High Tech offers us. As we embrace the devices and services that have become a part of our culture they begin to impact our lifestyles. We can't help it because you are digitally connected to global networks which harbour the Internet that breaks down your personal privacy door.

This means that you are no longer controlled of that privacy that entrance door offered. But the loss is not a bitter one, for the same Internet that impinges on your privacy has connected you to the world, bringing to you, right in your living hall samples of distant images and sounds that offer reflections of things either on your priority listing or things considered to be newsworthy or jaw dropping. Removing the fencing that isolates several communities from each other. Alerting you that now exists access to information, access to individuals, to groups to big data, to ideas, making the unreachable distant, a reachable click away.

Information usually taught at colleges and universities, come face to face with such abundance, offering a new concept to tradition access to information. Contemporary issues, necessary to shape your destiny, to remake you into an individual knowledgeable and worthy of an individual of an emerging,

Digital Technology era, with such stimulation to arouse your interest in issues in areas that you may not prioritize at college and university. Issues such as ; mass migration, elements of community growth and stability, lifestyles, habits and attitudes of the rich and powerful, foundation of community existence, just to name a few, offer easy access to you to examine at your own timing. To serve you to your best interest, a world of opportunities are opened up to you, as pages of technological landscape are flipped. An indication of generations' fascination with new products and services.

Generation Zoomers are much aware that they are born during the heat of Digital Technology development, they embrace the technology and show an unimaginable knowledgeable of the technology that you, the Zoomers have not only assimilate the digital culture but the technology has become your living lifestyles. Their eagerness, and knowledge of the technology portray them as the most to embrace the services of digital technology, on the efficiency use-level and willingness to embrace new products of digital technology, as well as engaged in Digital Technology .

As the technology motivates users to be "engaging" in preferred activities, users begin to self-discover their profile. Users self-identify their abilities and talents which begin to emerge. At social settings motivated by trusted friends, Generation Zoomers and Millennials soon recognize that they possessor can create digital content that others would like to share.

Users as they interact with friends, social group members, or community group members, members begin to take on the profile of content creators. Videos of interests are beamed to social groups of thousands of viewers. A clothe-line of an emerging entrepreneur is presented on location of posted on line sites on Social Media platforms. As the Internet links users globally, soon content of interest is shared globally in formats of picture, video and written words. Generations Zoomers and Millenniums demonstrate high level skill-sets in handling these various formats. Generations Boomers, are there to participate in the various processes.

Generation Bloomers use of excellent language skills in sentence structure, grammar usage, structural creation of content makes the presence of Generation Boomer invaluable. While Generation, Millenniums, posses a solid knowledge of applications of domestic application digital devices and services as well as applications in commercial uses. With their levels of digital maturity, their help in guiding socials groups to achieve a rational outcome in their related digital activities.

It is that technological changing world of digital innovations, scientists, innovators, technologist businessmen/women, government agencies speak of as the Digital Technology.

with electronic circuits that run devices that each carries an on-off switch. In urban cities the changing technological landscape is evident in Silicon Valley, California, Seattle Washington, USA and Toronto, Ontario, and Vancouver, British Columbia, Canada, to name a few cities. Digital innovations are used in offering services or in usable products in Canada and USA in a wide variety of consumer products and services, Industrial applications as well as in commercial services and products.

Devices and services that fit the concept of survival of the fittest begin to take roots in an authoritative dominance. Search engines deployed by Amazon, Yahoo and Google show leadership roles in their areas. The rise of Social Media platforms reinforced by the presence of the Internet, facilitate the need to transfer large quantity of data from location to location with digital precision and speed previously unknown. Clusters of firms working supportively to produce identified and agreed on products or services. Among the fascinating technology device that has become a cannot-do-without device, is the mobile phone. Never in the history of mankind, has there been a single device to which so many varieties of services have been attached for individual use. This device is the Mobile Phone. Below are some of the digital activities that manifest themselves in Western culture, in Canada and USA.

From these various activities such as, multiple network connections, increasing connection of humans and devices to networks via the internet globally, generate amazing products and services. The Emerging Social Platforms generating a new culture catering for social needs of individuals globally, is another digital activity bent to impact the digital culture.

The deployment of digital technology such as; Artificial Intelligence, digital devices, household appliances, commercial, as well as security systems which gather data and think as humans, are known as Internet of Things (IoT). When deployed in factories and are interconnected are commonly called "Industry Internet of Things, (IIoT). Both IoT and

IIoT figure much in moving functioning industry, towards Industry 4.0. The emerging Driverless Car, which sheds a new concept to the use of automobile is a digital product that is predicting to change the digital landscape of USA and Canada and other countries, globally

The use of Digital Ecosystem model, ensuring the production of digital products and services offers the possibility of transferring digital industries and culture globally, reinforced by the Exchange Theory.

The Digital Exchange Theory functions to pull business experts with skills and resources needed to create and deliver digital products and services encouraged by the main objective of increased financial benefits. The creation of digital environments, ie Smart Cities roamed by Driverless Automobiles and Smart Homes with appliances that talk to one another, as they producing data to predict efficient functioning of systems, these all have a place in the market place. The manufacturing of digital wearables motivates individuals to take more interest in their fitness levels. Users wear wrist bands, arm bands that gather personal related fitness data, these devices reminding users to step up their fitness training, or to continue the fitness activities, as required.

As these innovations of digital technology function efficiently, the individual has begun to experience an image change, an emerging digital image, reflecting social engagement, in recreational participation, he/she is magnetized to a digital device referred to as a "cannot-do-without", the mobile phone. As smart technology has been placed in devices, household equipment, the average citizenry enjoys a smart lifestyle, the use of the driverless car evidenced in revisiting a favourite of western culture, the automobile. As new technology finds place in the industry, creating a higher level of efficiency, existing equipment enjoys a digital make-over, generating jobs, and more jobs. Western culture has been shoved to higher elevations, as technology placed in most devices and equipment come together and functioned to fulfill manufacturers hope and desire.

The Mobile phone is unique in its use to access so many services a single component has never been in the history of human. When the user wants to interact with friends over Social Media platforms such as; Facebook, Instagram or WhatsApp, the use of the mobile phone is used for the job. When shopping for the best price on a product, the user accesses the sale price that variety of stores that sell such products. The user is going on a road trip outside of the city or within the confinement of the city, the use of Global Positioning Services, (GPS) services offer a high level direction to get to the destination, a small dent in cultural change but has significance in digital culture.

When you use the variety of services via your mobile phone, quite likely, you are connecting to different networks via the Internet. If the user responds by sending an email to someone, connection is being made to the recipient and offers the possibility of connecting to others within the recipient's networks, in effect users are expanding their connection on and on. That's the phenomenon of the Internet. As you connect to users within a service, there is the possibility that you increase your network, connection exponentially and possible offers access to others within that network.

The potential for existing analogue devices to be changed over to be driven by digital technology in the near future, 2021 will generate a multi billion-dollar industry in North America.

These devices also produce data which has multi-purpose uses. The numerous devices with the capability to produce data as well as to be connected to The Internet are labelled.*Internet of Things, (IoT).* The Internet which makes communication and delivery of informa-tion to be so important that messages and data delivered and received thousands of miles away within minutes is essential in the developing of firms that have deployed digital technology. As the capability of digital technology flourished, we are reminded that there is much to be done, and that those involved in decision making, may have a chance to make input in shaping new technology communities, so making the play field equally level for others. The unique opportunity exists now, so reminding us that there are some individuals of communities that usually have little connection and communication, decision to encourage deployment not only goes with the technology trending but also reminds us of basic component of our origins, connectivity within our communities.

Humans do have an active mind, how we select preferred items to act upon, is usually determined by where we are on our personal needs-listing and the kind of information that confronts us. If our origins, confront us and set our minds, to analyse, to act with the intent to re-discover things of interest, then it is quite likely we may act. We do not have to be interested in a specific topic or discipline to be engaged and so react towards such stimulus. Information presented via the internet and the media is presented so that it captures the viewer's interest and so encourages reaction.

The internet allows you to visit other point of views, often on your own time. Issues such as; under development, economic inequality, population explosion and mass migration which may be viewed as distant unrelated issues appeal to the sympathy cues that help to shape you as well as endowed in your human nature. So, when you see migrant kids separated from their parents, alone crying, a victim of poverty and as you assess the application of harsh, immigration laws, you may wish that only if you can offer some form of help. Humans have a curious mind, you just could rediscover that originally, we enjoy a connection that embraces the application of being "my brother's keeper," not only to wonder, but to examine, rationalize, and engage.

The connective access now brings again by networking, does offer the benefits therein, if needs be, to examine what is responsible for breaking the connection that once linked human to human. The motivation may not necessarily, an item on our personal preferential list, but may just be an opportunity made available, to examine to be placed on the checklist, when the time is right, through digital services.

Social Media Platforms which emerge to cater for an important part of human needs, social needs, have been emerging into a significant, communication platforms that service numerous sectors of the citizenry. With Facebook having daily users of about 1.5 billion, it has become a giant industry. Since data is fast becoming a commodity and users have personal data that business need, therefore, Facebook is an important partner of the business sector as well as asocial media platform, while Amazon recognizes that data exits in everything, so understanding the functional use of data in business application, no wonder, Jeff Bezos is viewed as the most contemporary, digital innovative person of our time.

As people of similar interests are drawn together and are connected, they share interests and issues, in effect social media groups have the capability to educate and empower groups globally, that have been dis-enfranchised.

The technology, Artificial Intelligence which is equipping machine to think as humans is a significant break-through in digital technology industry. The fascinating use of the technology in driverless automobile is a great example of deploying artificial intelligence sensors and computer systems to run automobile independent of humans in the driver's seat. Although, many strides have been made, there is much caution to be taken before a declaration of waving the banner of success.

Machine and devices driven by Artificial Intelligence systems do produce much data which offers some benefit to the user of the machine, the future looks bright for manufacturers, and others who may need to analyse the data produced for their business objective.

The whole concept of getting machine to think like a human and to produce data will have significant impact how smart machine are being viewed and applied within a changing technological landscape.

Artificial Intelligence technology is already deployed in industry, rooted soundly in household application, and widely used in utility systems in *Smart Cities.*

Examples are; water system, transport system, education systems. In the use of wearable devices, such as wristband, the technology is used to monitor the user's heart rate and so alerts the individual if he needs to be rushed to the hospital to seek emergency, medical care as his heart rate increases drastically. Similarly, a wearable device can inform the user that he/she needs to go to the gym to maintain his/her level of fitness.

Innovators have compared business environments positioned to foster the growth of digital business and elements required to support the production of products and services as "*Digital Ecosystems*" which parallel the biological ecosystems. In essence, Digital Ecosystems consist of a cluster of businesses that offer supportive services in the production of digital products and services are live Digital Ecosystems which have all the necessary infrastructure to facilitate products and services from the start to the final product/service completion going all the way to the final sale of the products/services.

The Digital Ecosystems are not only springing up in Western culture but is springing up globally. That is a part of the digital technology global transformation. A significant consumer's area in which Artificial Intelligence is used in impacting culture is the use of "fitness trackers" to monitor the user's level of fitness. These wearable devices designed to be worn on the wrists or around the waist of users empower the users to take responsibility for personal fitness. Each device is designed and carried more than one fitness objectives. In this way users can monitor; the body recovering from stress, heart rate or other organs need monitoring. In digital numbers, level of expected fitness is displayed, showing the level of fitness so, reminding the user that actions are needed to be taken.

Most of these fitness device solutions produced data, manufacturers hooked them-up online as they sent relevant data to manufacturers and to their personal users. The application of these keep-fit trackers has much application in present and future uses as they relay information to users within the timeframe in which they are being used. As the user is cycling, jogging, "pumping iron" or swimming, information about the level of fitness is sent to the user in real time. Fitness trackers can even monitor the users' sleeping patterns, light sleep or deep sleep. It is normally held that fitness contributes towards healthy living, acceptable level of fitness is usually sought to be achieved and maintained.

Within the urban city, the home is the basic unit that encourages family togetherness, security, and family legitimacy. The individual works in a setting where the machinery and devices are "smart". He lives in a city where the utility systems are driven by smart Artificial Intelligence sensors and smart systems.

During leisure, in the plaza, at home or awaiting his/her turn in the doctor's office the mobile phone comes to facilitate some form of engagaged activity as such time-slot usually is a non-assigned. All around the individual, digital technology is impacting him/her. Technology is used to improve the quality of life; digital technology seems to have been doing just that. So it is within logics that innovators would create, The Smart Home.

Basic to the Smart Home is the Internet, we need the Internet because the Internet of Things and other devices are widely used in Smart Homes receiving data, creating data, and transmitting data. The Internet is the lifeline for the Internet of Things, all of these possible smart devices possess the capability to be accessed remotely, offer changes to the ways tasks are done. Some household appliances and devices that are undergoing digital make-over driven by digital sensors are microwaves oven, refrigerator, television, lamps etc. will be the future norm.

Smart home has the capability to allow the home user to moni-tor his/her home remotely. Such facial recognition camera analyses the face of a suspicious individual and accurately indicates if the individual is an intruder and is not welcome to that home. While the other individuals present, each is given a pass.

Changing Technology Landscape impacting the

Individual and Digital Culture

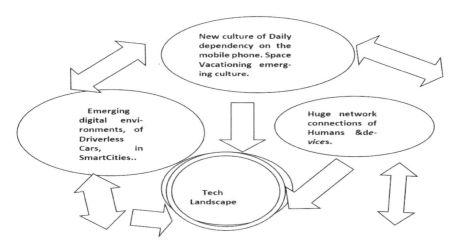

Infographics 2-1 showing Digital Technology impacting change in significant areas of Western
Culture.

Consumers' purchasing attitudes in purchasing digital products are very important to marketing experts, as citizens respond positively. to digital products and services. The use of these services and products are well entrenched in the economy and cultural practices.

Elements such as music, film. Internet communication, formats such as; email, various uses of "texting" take on different formats, the digital format. While technology such as; the various uses of the mobile phone and functioning of it's portability reinforces its purpose in the society. The Tablet, desktop and laptop, computer technologies are the roots that offer strength and drive the emerging digital technology.

The discovery of accurate analysis of big data has application to generate habits as well as to be used to direct organization effectiveness demonstrates that the production of data by devices, equipment and by humans all connected to the network of people and things has significant uses now and far in the future.

Because you have been commercially molded to respond to products and services of our highly commercialized society and as long as you live in any of the continents of this modern world, unavoidably you are hooked up to services or products offered by providers. Such connection breaks down boundaries.

Through the Internet you may be connected to a service provider in your city, that service provider may be connected to another service provider or client in another city of your country which in turn is connected to another service provider in another country thousands of miles away. Through the connection of the Internet, it is quite possible that the individual or the service provider who has a web site or an Internet address thousands of miles away can connect to you at almost any time to influence your life, so impacting your lifestyle, creating a different lifestyle. But the impact is not a scary one, it's a situation to embrace, to explore, every situation comes with a form of risk, it's for you to be alert of any danger within.

Many products or services that are available to be purchased, has a provider at the other end using the Internet as means of sending and receiving data. This is done by sending such information via the Internet. While you at one of the devices use one of these devices; desktop, or laptop computers as

well as others, receive[1] data related to the business. Just think of the electronically, connected world. As you use these services you become a part of the global connections.

FIGURE 1-2 Digital Technology has a place in all areas of lifestyle.

The influence is so significant that the supplier can tailor products and services just for you because your analysed data let him know what your purchasing habits are. But as our needs are now hooked up to numerous services and products, there are other users whose intention is subjectively motivated. Their purpose is not to make a buck or two off you, neither to offer help to those who need help but as they gather your personal information, such information has become a 'gold mine' for them when such data is sold in great quantity.

Great quantity of data is sold to data analytic firms that analyse data,and figure out the commercial use of the accumulated data, including a price. This practice is slowly gathering globally.

---

[1]   Device, such as mobile phone or a computer devices such as a desk top, or lap top computers, high speed internet along with availability of Wi-Fi as well as other services.

We in the West enjoy freedom of speech. Spoken and written words released on our various media platforms may consider to be treasonous, if were released in some countries. Technology used in commercial products acceptable to everyone in the West such technology may be of "interest" to others in foreign countries. If the individual demonstrates expert knowledge in certain technology that individual/s may be of 'global importance'. Your 'global importance' translilate in the form of personal data can be transmitted globally because you are a part of the connected world.

Whether you like it or not you are now an "Individual connected to the world". The digital era has changed the philosophical thought once held by some thinkers who argued that "Man is alone in the universe," now we have to admit that he is globally connected and has access to information as never before in the existence of mankind. As he has access to others as well as their information, others have access to him/her too. The transforming technology landscape is timely changing the individual from a lay back individual to an 'engaging' individual. He recognizes the difference between sitting and just listening to wise men who impart their knowledge to those who are fashioned to be listeners. The emerging individual is developing a mindset of his own he/she is also slipping into digital make-over.

As data is at his fingers' tips, he has become knowledgeable, great libraries that previously accessible only by selected few, now is accessible to those who want to. Often you are only aware that others have access to you when you look at your *digital markers*. Everyone creates digital markers as they use digital devices to respond to information or to send digital information. Digital markers are comparable to your footprints that you make when you walk in the snow or on a soft, water-wet soil, surface. This allows someone to see your prints and trace the footprints back to you. Similarly, the use of digital devices within the networks that you are now connected to, create digital footprints. This marker can be used by others to get to you. Some of the people who may want to get to you may not be those who you want to access you for positive reasons. But what are the elements left behind that allow others to access you? Your telephone number, whether the mobile or line phone number, if they get into the hands of scammers easy access to you is available.

With cleverly, woven tales used to influence the receiver at the other end of the line. In Canada and the USA millions of dollars have been scammed especially, from senior citizens. Even to the extent that the events become so unbearable, that some take their lives. It is of importance to know what happens to your data when you purchase products or services from firms. Your personal information is stored in the computer data base of that firm.

There are computer hackers who are motivated to crack the security of some companies as they possess information that could be sig-nificant. So, the suggestion is when you pass on your personal data to Customer Service you need to enquire of the kind of security that will protect your personal data. The use of the mobile phone in taking pictures, is now a fad. There are numerous people who frolic in taking personal pictures ,posting them on Social Media within the moments of having fun especially at parties. As many "drop their guards" and so allow others to enter their personal space where they involved in activity like taking the victim's personal picture, without the victim knowing of the intended uses.

With the available of computer software, pictures can be altered to cause the individual social embarrassment. Such pictures could be used to generate monetary incentives that may impact you. Pictures can be altered to create an entirely new person.

Evidence has recently shown that each individual's personal data in great quantity has significant value to data analytic firms. When you take out an account with these social media platforms, your person data that you are required to supply has much monetary value when sold to data analytic firms. The data is analysed with certain objectives in mind.

The end-result is that the analysed data sold to firms that create products, tailored-packages, and even retail depots to lure customers to purchase their services or products. Firms that sell your data or use it for monetary purposes will suggest that they have got permission to use the individual's data. Without being aware, you may have given permission for the use of your personal data when you check " yes" in the box in reference to 'cookies'. It always makes sense to inquire what purpose your data will be used for. You may be aware that at attempts to influence consumer purchasing habits are not new strategies. During the analogue era, a variety of advertisements have been used to influence consumers' purchasing habits, this strategy is carried over to the digital era.

Consumers, within the digital, era can be smart shoppers since this era embraces the concept of smartness in numerous areas of the culture. They may shop wisely by comparing similar products/services sold at shops for qualities, prices, intended uses, making sure they carry the features you really expected, such information is next to you in your mobile phone. For the first time in human history your personal connection with networks creates a social platform that allows humans even at home to satisfy a significant need level, social needs.

Most social scientists may agree that humans are social beings. So, as humans gather in great numbers at social venues that host parties, concerts, sports events, those who cannot be on locations to enjoy these events can stay in their homes and on social networks such as Facebook, Instagram, WhatsApp may interact with other users so satisfying that social needs. Our connection to our devices has become a fad, in such way that some individuals will use only one name brand of phone. Well, personal selection of a product in this case, a mobile phone is a democratic choice and is a democratic way. But as we are connected to other devices such as our laptop and desk top computers, software programs like word processing have become a billion-dollar market.

When computers are sold with software programs already installed from one manufacturer, then others who want to have a part of the money-making market, argues that when one firm is monopolizing the market with its word processing software others are shut out of that market. Such monopoly may have little impact on the individual connected to the networks if the pricing of the product is reasonable. But it is difficult for consumers to determine an accurate pricing when there is no alternate seller some may argue.

Although it can be argued that the more sellers there are in the market, the greater the potential for price to be lowered, that is a solid argument. So, we can agree, that having more sellers in the market for word processing software, is essential. But also essential   is for others to maintain there survival techniques. Truly, others have come and have gone within a short time.

Engineers and technologists associated with crafting the systems and devices, understand the competence needs of users. They know how to motivate users especially when they lack competence skills required to use the systems efficiently, as well as related devices within the networks. Functioning devices and systems to be used within the networks are crafted to be "user friendly". User friendliness reduces anxiety and frustration. These men and women designed and built the systems and devices to meet these emotional needs of users. Users also need guidance and protection from national predators as well as global predators.

The user must be aware that he/she is no longer and individual alone on planet, earth but is hooked up with others emerging with a proactive mindset that is functionally alert that his/her data is of global importance. That he is globally connected to the world, so the potential to be accessed locally as well as globally is there. So, initiative should be deployed to ensure that his/her digital gate is locked, and only made accessible by permission, when the user wants to enable the user to function well in the digital landscape I am proposing a **3-Point Model** that will be useful as you function in a digitally connected world in which you are hooked-up to.

HERE IS A 3-POINT MODEL FOR USE IN

DIGITALLY CONNECTED NETWORKS

(1) As you interact with users, service providers of any networks be careful what kind of digital markers you leave behind that can be used to get back to you.

(2) As you socialized with users on-location or on line be conscious of those who are around you and what their objectives and actions are.

(3) When you are not certain of a decision you are about to make, always ask, "What if...?" If the generated response is negative, follow your "gut feeling" that directs you to pro-tect yourself.

If you need help, work with a trustworthy, support person, preferably a family member, someone that you can access easily and who you can depend on to guide i making the best related decisions that you may make. See infographics of the 3-Point Model on pg. # 53.

The importance of maintaining a consistent Wireless Fidelity (Wi- Fi) for connection to the internet is very important. The use of the internet as necessary in maintaining connection with local users as well as global users of networks must be recognized by the user. The portability of the mobile phone enabling connection within your personal networks as well as the global networks from the start of your waking hours to the time when you lie down to sleep offers priority usage by many who send and receive messages away from home and offices.

In countries where democracy is practised in a limited way, access to networks usually awaken their minds as they realized that they could receive and send information. This could open new ways of thinking, interacting with peers near and in distant lands as well as enabling the individual to be positioning himself or her-self to communicate with top management almost unheard of under the old analogue communication model. Access to top management was almost an impossible act due to a vertical structure that related, communication model has designed to prevent easy access to top management. Often technology that requires to get the individual hooked up to networks, is not available in developing countries and even in what is referred to as remote areas in developed countries such as USA and Canada.

As digitalization of services and products impact our Western society, consumers' attitudes as well as industry demands encourage the continuation of these products and services. We see a change of focus from Silicon Valley and Washington in USA as the cities of digital, technology 'starts-up', now rival by Toronto, a technological city of Canada in technology job production. A form of globalization takes effect as the politics of rejection of immigrants to work in the USA allows immigrant engineers and technologists especially from Asia to select Toronto, Canada as the technology city to work. Emphasis is placed upon the prevention of giant technology companies of the USA from buying out the new start-ups reinforces the possibility of continual existence of solid technology hub in Toronto.

With support of universities such as University of Toronto, University of Ottawa, and University of Waterloo providing programs comparable to the best in Western society, reinforces the possibility of long life in technology impacting at the local level as well as at the global level.

The evolution of social organizations to participates in training community members to understand and use video cameras to expose human right abuses in their communities. To guide and help others to exist acceptable human rights levels. While some groups have conttributed their share in helping people to pursue their personal goals at acceptable human rights level. Discriminatory practices of police officers in the U.S.A motivate community members globally to use social media to communicate and plan supportive demonstrations supporting the "cause".

But the changing technological landscape is not only limited to consumer products and evolving of social media platforms, but significant impact is also made on industrial and commercial products. The way information is processed and stored in office setting is more efficient and user friendly. New technology has created a new emerging culture, as driverless automobiles although in the experimental stages is set to create a new driving culture. Digitalization creates added features and efficiency to existing technology such as placing robots in more use in commercial situations. The creation of giant organizations such as Amazon, the giant company makes the owner, Jeff Bezos among the richest men in the world, having a net worth of$165.6 billion USD. Jeff Bezos surely, has made a solid statement in this digital world.

The existence of flagship firms such as Microsoft and Google, Apple and, Tesla as well as others suggest, the impact of firms transforming the technological landscape. For economy to thrive and do well in this Digital Revolution Era, a solid digital infrastructure must be proven and be reliable. As noticed in impacting economies such as USA, Canada, and England, digital infrastructure consists of high-speed Internet. Devices to access the Internet such as; desktop or laptop computers, along with reliable Wi-Fi. A reliable high speed Internet service infrastructure is a must.

As innovators' ideas are transformed into goods and services which make great impact on the market, could their wishes be that regulations which can significantly affect features of a product or service may be subjected to minimal governmental control? We see very little regulations placed upon the mobile phone. Many of you may remember the concern that the mobile phone emits radioactive waves which are harmful to humans and much preventive measures were suggested. Now-a-days, especially in USA and Canada not much is heard about radioactivity and the relatedness to the mobile phone.

Such awareness is very necessary to educate, especially young emerging users. Recognition that service providers are needed who will ensure high speed Internet service, as data transfer is an important element of the digital technology transformation landscape is essential to reinforce continued existence.

As high-quality Internet service is also an element that encourages efficiency, portable, mobile phones usually capture the eyes of consumers. and are basics to our technological landscape. They are part of the information put on websites, some may suggest that is why these products or services have so much applications and many multi-uses .

The mobile phone has significant impact on the technological landscape and has a part of the global identity among things that identify humans and trending lifestyles. For example, as clothing is something that all humans wear, the mobile phone is a device that humans carry with them everywhere to stay connected in a digitally connected world. It has become a part of "the must have, must use" trending.

In the history of humans, there is not a single device or object, as the mobile phone that offers so many services, hooked up to it. Although some of the services are at the initial stage hooked up and require much fine tuning. Definately, the mobile phone has found a niche in our culture. As the aggregate efficiency of the phone is developed, an area of service that consumers could benefit from, is more wider monitoring human health, to offer basic health information. To monitoring certain health conditions bringing quick information to the user.

So, in situations of pending emergency, the device alerts the user to respond quickly to seek medical help. There are wrist watches on the market used to monitor health conditions. As maintaining a healthy self is always a priority to the average citizenry, may be the watch or the phone is the possible route for the future.

A functioning mobile phone seems to be growing closer and closer to the hearts of millennial users. Although depending on online communication has much advantage, this form of communication should not replace face to face interaction with others. As it is a part of our nature to connect face-to-face with humans. This will be a sad day if Digital Technology separates us from one another.

Since the cost of an average mobile phone is less than the cost of most computers, the phone functions as basic connector to the networks. But probably the social network platforms offer much social satisfactions to users who intended to just connect on line, those just want to connect globally or making initial connection for later face to face interaction could be a main purpose. Once the connection is made other benefits follow.

You may use all or one of the social media platforms such as;

1. **Facebook, Instagram, WhatsApp, You Tube and Twitter to connect and communicate with a group or with an individual of shared interest. The absence of a close face to face presence of just only on line communications eliminate threatening situations that sometimes "face to face" interaction brings. In effect, don't be surprised that counselors and sociologists suggest that factors that affect individuals such as; fear, nervousness, caused the presence of face-to-face interaction are significantly reduced.**

2. Speed and clarity are elements attached to digital communication; these allow the user to communicate with others on selected media platform thousands of miles away.

3. Research shows that users connect with Social Media platforms to express empathy to friends, with family members distant away. Similarly, in turn receives expressed empathy from friends and family members distant away.

4. The use of Social Media platforms, supporting network members to mobilize people to support issues at the global levels to effect community changes is a fireball in the making.

5. Just find your participating voice right at Social Media platform.

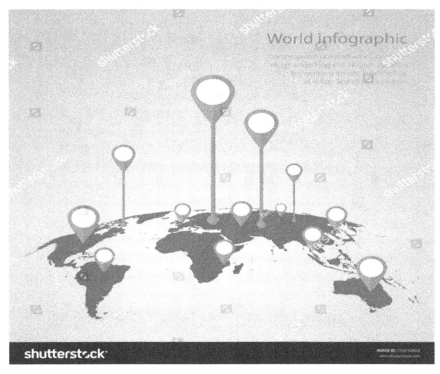

Figure 1-2 Infographic showing Social Media is a part of the global digital connection.

Since the user has access to posting and sending messages within his/her network, issues of personal interests can be identified and shared. There are spin-off groups who have set out to help those who need help.

CHAPTER 2

~

Rise of Social Media Platforms

Figure2-1 platforms and areas of impact on culture. Shutterstock infographics.

Organization **psychologists must have been** really happy as they observe the evolution of Social Media Platforms, as demonstrated by multi-billion clientele users of Facebook, closely followed by Twitter, Instagram, WhatsApp, and others. The evolution is not strange as many organizational psychologists embrace the current concept that within the pyramid of needs, social needs have their place on the Needs Pyramid Model, as a Middle Order Needs. So, suggesting the importance of those needs within an individual, to be satisfied.

We see these users of Social Media, embracing individual users allowing them to connect with friends via the Internet. Users soon recognize that they can have personal chats with someone whom they choose to. They can socialize even on an intimate level. Access to individuals with similar concerns, mutually, receives or sends gestures of empathy that offer some degree of solutions to a user who needs some form of help.

As Social Media platforms offer each user a free account, this concept is not a usual practice in business. As this has become a practice of such business model, strikes a note to be noticed by other firms. The implication is that a firm can stay successful in business, without functioning to maximize its profits. As successfully demonstrated by the Social Media, platforms that offer free membership for exchange of access to members' personal, data, free media accounts, is a great strategy to lore potential membership to exchange resources.

Such strategy could be an indication that business leaders do apply moral principles in decision making, a new building block for the reconstruction of a new digital world. Access to the user, personal information has to be authorized upon signing up for membership. Interestingly, the value of personal data sold by the owner does not have any significant market value, an individual unit on the emerging, commercial market to the user, about $ 0.60 to $1.70 USD. But when data is sold in great number as in millions, then your personal data along with others have eye-opening values. Like a bate thrown at a fish in the ocean, the digital cookie is offered to each future candidate. When it is accepted, brings the future candidate user to that focal point as permission is given to use the user's personal data.

The user gets his social needs looked after while the owner meets his monetary objective. This is a significant example of the Exchange Theory at work in the business management. Both parties seem to benefit at a high level in the exchange process.

As Social Media demonstrates that this is an element that is here to make a visible change in the technological landscape, it also demonstrates the possibility of it evolving into a pipe line emptying information into **Disappearing Information of Horizon** as well as a media sending information that has an unlimited life-span.

The daily use of Twitter by 45th USA president to deliver all kind of information to 125 million people in USA and another 25 million in Canada plus the large audience throughout the world must have created much demanding weight in authenticity of information delivered. The limitation of the number of characters that put limits upon what can be written often is a hindrance in communication. Because user like the President, sends his messages daily, before an appropriate response is posted, a new tweet is posted that may even demand attention than the previous tweet. In effect, those bits of information have been knocked, over into the information horizon, to stay dormant, although can be resurrected for several uses.

As the media emerges, dominant and frequent topics tweeted may be the way in creation of systematic methods of communicating on issues of interests for the sender and the recipients, as evidenced in frequency of tweeting on political topics. So, creating a quick response and allowing citizens to respond to issues on polices as well as political leaders reward, in creating communication-links with constituents' members.

We must remind ourselves that technology is usually embraced to improve our lives. As it emerges, caution should be taken that the change is upward not downward as in the case with the uses of basic logics and basic, standardized communication language.

It is noticeable, when tweeting, there is a need to remind the sender of consistency of his/her argument that is being made. Evidence shows that the concept of consistency has taken a back seat especially when it comes to political leadership communication. As the technology of Artificial Intelligence is fine tuned and so gets better, the concept of consistency could be programmed in the package to alert the user that consistency is being ignored, based upon previous tweets posted.

Maybe, we could argue that the processes of "tweeting" is still in the initial stage and its evolution will remedy that problem. In ref-erence to written language in the analogue days, there was the refer-ence dictionaries which were used as standard to justify word usage, spelling, origin of words, parts of speech to which each word can be defined. No tweets are subjected to the scrutiny of any standard writ-ten communication.

For example, to place emphasis on a word, when tweeting, that word is written in upper case letters. In the use of basic, standard English communication, such a practice is literally incorrect. But as Social Media platforms evolve, such practice could be standardized, as such use can cause much confusion for young beginning users of 'tweets' as they are at the stage of assimilating what comes to them as standard and procedures. This practice is also evident with "tweeting". We must remember to guide our young users as they grow to be participants of an ever emerging changing, digital world.

Social Media communication seems to offer easy access to political leaders as well as have the provision to generate quick responses. The long wait on political leaders to use the tradition news media to address an issue is now replaced or preceded by couple minutes tweets awaiting the user as he/she rises from personal sleep. Digital Technology is associated with the fast movement of data, written language is data, so it is expected that written language is delivered to the audience now at a rapid speed.

But there seems to be a connection between twitter and the aver-age person who uses the electronic media. As users embrace Social Media platforms, they leave behind digital markers that others can use to trace back to you the users. Just like footprints in snow or foot prints made on a soft, soil surface on a rainy day can lead back right to the user's doorsteps. These markers could lead others to the user's private world. For you must remember that as much as you need to protect your digital markers, others can leave digital markers that will trap the user, by making access available to the scammer.

In this case, the digital markers could just lead you to digital platforms such as a speech on the television, or digital platform such as; tradition media, TV or Radio, News Magazines, daily newspaper. Charismatic speakers or leaders have thousands and sometimes millions of followers who follow them, some of these leaders are super stars.

Others are; sports personalities, politicians, billionaires, followers are so attracted to them that they will listen to them, or respond positively to them. Such followers are being magnetized and are compelled to demonstrate some form of responses to statements that digital superstars put out in the public domain. These responses must be scrutinized before placed or released on the media as scammers could just access such information or modify the information to reflect their own perspective.

The power of luring followers from one media platform to the other media platform is seen in modern day political leadership communication. Early in the morning a tweet is posted while there is a continuation of the similar message at a meeting or rally or of some media platforms, placing emphasis on similar messages posted earlier. The use of excellent communication skills to influence others as well as having influenced listeners who accept leaders' spoken messages as absolute truth. This is a carried over from the days of the analogue when trust is placed upon tradition media communication platforms as instruments of truth.

Followers will respond to the speaker. As the mindset of trusting kicks in, the influencer, takes over and the listeners are as if they are hypnotized. That's the moments when group psychology reinforces the desired behaviour, they respond in one voice. Many of you may remember the chant, "Lock her up! Lock her up! Lock her up!" They know the news stories that surround such chant, but no one cares for justification. The influencer has hypnotized his followers, as he speaks in the kind of vernacular cemented in their lives.

It is this trust that although several red flags are fluttered within an area of reasonable understanding, the tendency is not to evaluate but to accept and act upon the suggestion. So, communication principles, such as absolute truth, facts, consistency and standard, language principles are thrown out the window.

Facebook is designed to accommodate effectively, written and picture communication formats which impact the world significantly. On these platforms, "a picture's worth more than a thousand words" has significant applications. Especially, with users of mobile phones. As mobile phones are attached with digital cameras, the user is motivated to shoot and post their message on Social Media platforms.

Again, Facebook provides an area of social needs in which humans require satisfaction. With more than 1.5 billion users daily suggest the transformational impact Facebook has made on the technological landscape. The impact of Facebook in the future is alarming when we realize that almost .5 of the population of the world is not yet con-nected to the Internet Since the basic equipment is available, which is basic mobile phone and high-speed internet, the existence of the Digital Ecosystem makes digital globalization a possibility.

Facebook has already lay down the foundation of attraction to users as they are encouraged to the Social Media to express themselves, such expression often draws acknowledgement. Oprah Winfrey in one of her talk shows suggests that 'acknowledgement' is an area of an individual's life he/she seeks to satisfy. This does not apply to women alone, but men as well. As a matter of facts, in several areas. In a commercial world where consumers are expected to pay for everything except for air and sometimes water, no users may take out an account "free of cost." But social media offers this benefit to users.

Such practice makes good business sense, or even points to moral responsibility which needs to practice more often, within the business world. Here is another example of the application of **Digital Exchange Theory**, the user gets a free account that offers satisfaction for his/ her social needs while the specific Social Media gets access to the user's personal information, **both parties are benefited from the interaction.**

But Facebook is not losing out on such decisions, for in 2018 it is estimated that Facebook generates a revenue of S55,838 million U.S.D in that year. Both parties share in the benefits, users do not pay for the services while Facebook utilize users' data. This application of the **Digital Exchange Theory may not what social scientist envisage but may be a starting point for others to think examine.** Social media bosses must be commended for such a "starting point", there could be a follow-up to create a next mutual benefit in the chain of decision making, **by looking into equitable shared Distribution of Profits.**

Facebook core market is focused on USA, Canada, and the United Kingdom. Since Facebook has access to data when analysed, can generate significant marketing outcomes as well as for use to **generate administrative** efficiency, With that goal in mind, recent uses of individuals' data without their permission caused great concern to the extent that Mark Zuckerberg was summoned to USA, Congress to report on what his company will do to protect users' data. This comes about as a former employee, of Cambridge Analytical, a data analytical company decided to go public revealing that millions of personal data of Social Media users have been used by executives of the incumbent USA, president to influence constituents voting decisions.

The access of personal data has come into discussions. In effect, Mr Zuckerberg, founder, and Chief Executive Officer, of a powerful social media platform had been called to U.S.A, Congress to answer questions from members of Congress. Mr. Zuckerberg was very supportive and indicated his willingness to make changes to protect users 'personal data was remarkable.

As Social Media and other media formats collect personal data on users, application for uses becomes noticeable. In Canada, a private firm is partnering with the Federal Government of Canada by getting researchers to collect large data on social media users. Their data is analysed to look for dysfunctional tendencies, manifested in selected community members, such as suicidal tendences and the potential to hurt themselves. Application of data mining and using the analysed data as solutions for social or behavior problems suggest the range of applications of uses of "Big Data" mining and analytics. There are some politicians in England who believed that the use of "Big Data" analysed to impact voting in England to generate exit from the European union, is significant application of use of data to generate such outcome.

As Social Media is like many other digital media that is impacting the technological landscape, innovators and consumers purchasing attitudes will also factor in the directions that Social Media platform will go. It has already shaping the culture significantly. Like the geological earth movements that forged planet earth into visible continents, so is Social Media shaping earth into visible and new culture, called Social Media platforms.

The evolution of Social Media platforms as used to offer satisfaction to social needs of humans represent the potential for global growth; as demonstrated in multi-billion users of Facebook, Twitter, Instagram, WhatsApp, and others. The evolution is not strange as many organizational psychologists embrace the current concept that within the pyramid of needs, social needs have its place as a middle order need.

We see these users of the Social Media, embracing individual users allowing them to connect to friends via the Internet. Users recognize that they can have personal chats with someone whom they choose to. They can socialize even on an intimate level. Access to individuals with similar concerns receives or sends gestures of empathy.

Is this a win, win situation for the user of the social media, as it is strongly held that everyone is responsible for his or her behaviour, yet there is a tendency that interaction within a social setting can sig-nificantly impact the individual's behaviour to the extent that he/she deviates from the usual normative behaviour. The use of social media platforms in postings of pictures, posting personal statements, tweets are a part of your digital image. As a casual user of Facebook remarked in his posting, "Whatever your pictures suggest of you, that is what you are, and how you want to be treated".

Social Media platforms are also a digital phenomenon that is signiificantly offering a make-over to the individual in our transforming digital landscape. There is no reference standard at present, your value systems is your standard of reference. Interestingly, as users focused on their personal cues, they may just have to think of those young folks who are still who are in their formative years of creating their value systems and need some guidance. You the mature person may just function as a role model for others, "hold you head high" while social behavior, for other may just be accepting your display of social conduct as acceptable standard of conduct. Often, we do undergo changes or being impacted by changes, without being aware of its impact and the ripple effects of our social conduct.

Similarly, you are being exposed to negatives spin-off from the evolving digital era which will surely impact you. There are scammers and hackers and others who may even try to steal your identity. Such effects may not necessarily define you but will impact you somehow. Opportunities for the skilled residents to create a service or product, get it to the market so that it will make you a millionaire, is a possibility in a vibrant, technological economy. If this happens to you such events can even significantly define your identity.

As digital innovations, impact the changing technological land-scape, you the citizens, unavoidably experiencing, new eye-catching devices. New lifestyles, the choice of selective, visual imagery, the opportunity to experience situations that smart technology offers. Immerse yourselves in emotion, heart-throbbing, personal and group events, examine and make purchases of consumer products that main-tain or upgrade your digital imagery.

As you attached yourselves to digital innovations that have become a part of your daily lifestyle, you may just have to be careful as you interact with others. When you go through these processes, at work, in social settings or at consumer setting, you are creating a digital identity. But this identity keeps changing for everyone is functioning in a changing, new world. A changing world that will shake-up or shake-down the world not like an H-bomb but quietly like the Industrial Revolution.

One of the negative side effects of the industrial revolution is some cities in Europe were covered with soot generated from chim-neys of factories in operation. The soot polluted the air that residents had to breathe. That was one of the significant negative effects of the Industrial Revolution.

Similarly, you are being exposed to negatives spin-offs, from disruptors of digital technology systems which will surely impact you. These are scammers and hackers and others who may even try to steal your identity, will use Social Media platforms at all means to create havoc in your life. Telephone communication usually a media of trust, now we have entered an era of mistrust and fear of people standing close to us. For someone peeking over your shoulder could allow the individual to memorise your password to your bank account so drain it. Responding to verbal instructions on the phone could generate similar effect. As the world is now at your doorstep, the fragility of love is used as a weapon against those who carry a trusting heart.

Such effects may not necessarily define you but may restrict your decisions that you make, how you interact with others as you utilize digital services. Opportunities for the skilled residents to create a service or product, get it on the market that will make them a millionaire, is a possibility, in a vibrant technological economy. If this happens to you such events may significantly impact your digital identity.

CHAPTER 3

Emerging Technology
A Place of Hidden Chaos

Two basic components that usually come along with most form of revolutions are; "change and chaos." Both components are usually a function of "cause and effect" principles, meaning as a result of the initiatives of the revolution, change and chaos occur. There is no doubt that the occurring changes in the technology landscape are evident in communication, business, lifestyle, Social Media and others are results of the emerging digital technology. In contrast to "change," chaos as evident south of the border, is not related to the "Cause and Effect" principle but seems to find its roots in "*accommodation*" principle. Accommodation is a principle of the *Digital Exchange Theory*.

This principle suggests that individuals are socially drawn together to participate in shared benefits. This is exemplified in a construction site where a variety of workers are attracted to contribute their skills in creating a project with a common objective, "making some money" i.e. via a salary. This is evidenced in situations such as an industrial or commercial projects where workers come together to pool their skills to complete an industrial factory or a commercial building, to set-up production lines to produce products or services to be sold to consumers. The foreach participant, working co-operatively is that each receives a weekly or bi-weekly salary, or whatever payment format agreed upon. Subtle chaos can be generated within this group and be accommodated based upon the intended goals of the group does not seem to generate concern to political leadership in our Western world sometimes functions as a model for others emerging, developing countries, set leadership aspiration and guidance for leaders of developing countries, while young minds of kids in the formative years, are impacted by leadership, normative behavior is shaped. Therefore, leadership roles are expected to encourage stability and generate behavior that will prevent chaos.

People in the Western culture, embrace the relatively chaos-free USA campaign and transfer of power during the presidential election of U.S.A as well as the transfer of power from Prime Minister to another Prime Minister in Canada. But the digital tech-nology seems to downplay a mild disruption in the democratic polit-ical system in USA.

If the technology hubs of Toronto, Canada, Washington, and Silicon Valley claim to be the most technology innovation in the West, with the ability to turn out new technology to serve consumers needs as well as to find solutions to existing digital technology problems, yet the enemy country has created a degree of discomfort to the digital technology landscape. Specifically, by invading Social Media platforms. Cyber watchers claim that the enemy creates disruptions by deploying false posting on Facebook in favor of their preferred, presidential candidate, with the intent to swing votes towards the enemy preferred candidate.

One would think that if the discovery of interference to cause disruption is made known during the 2016 presidential election, then policies would be in place to prevent any other interference.

But the citizenry of the West must have been shocked in 2019, during Mueller Testimony before Congress, claiming that a foreign nation at "that very moment is interfering in the USA presidential election. Another implication which is significant too, is portability of transferring Digital Ecosystems globally, to create start-ups to produce goods and services. The technology also suggests that military and economic power offer strength to powerful countries to stand out as the modern Samson. Digital technology has the potential to bring to the arena of power, another power source, digital disruption technology.

Most Americans feel that another country has made input of disruption during the 2016 presidential election. Journalists claim that disruption is initiated via the use of the internet by planting false news stories of rumors on media such as Facebook and Twitter with the intent to impact thinking and decision making of citizens of intended countries. This disruption is so subtle that it takes over 2 years of Federal Bureau of Investigation to find out that such disruption had occurred.

To create chaos those involved need to know how the individual or group of people will respond to certain situations, then creating situations with cues for the respondents to respond to. Investigation of the ruling government leadership which has continued over a year caused significant division among pepper-tempered opposing politicians of major two parties.

New York Times among many reputable news media claims that the incumbent president, within 2 years of his ruling has made more than 10,000 false claims, others use harsh terms such as lies. Facts as reliable source of information must have reliability attached to facts. For when the facts are distorted, disruption can be generated. Especially, as we move into an era where data is viewed as important commodity, reliability and facts may be significant elements that help to determine the value of some data.

As power of video communication, specifically as used on television brings cultural practices right in our living hall, since much of our down time is used to watching television. We in our Western society easily identify with some of cultural practices shown on television. The impact of seeing imagery that you like and wanting to associate with those imagery, after a time you develop a feeling of belongingness, belonging to that culture.

We see a shift of rapid delivery of information via social media using such media to criticize the president. On one occasion, such criticism generates a response that he tweets negatively about the author, nine times in one day.

Two days after the release of the negative tweets, the act con-tinues. As if the chaotic mood of the White House is not enough, the White House which is the mouthpiece of the president releases information referring to the names of high profile past workers of FBI and CIA. Such information generates disruption for those seek-ing information from live reliable sources, that is, former reliable workers of government departments who have firsthand knowledge of needed information. The issue created was that their security access issued by the White House have been taken away. Among them were Ex-Security Chief, CIA, John Brennan, and Ex-Security Chief, FBI, James Clapper. All of whom had criticize the president using the tradition media as well as the Social Media networks. Here again is subtle chaos, as these formerly high-ranking ex-work-ers function as human resource for government departments that they are so skilled in. The relevance to Canadian citizenry, is that Canadian usually feel that changes that occur in U.S.A within the long run will also take place in Canada.

A principle of digital technology is the ability of the format to send out quickly impacting messages that generate quick responses.

But if the implication is, "If you criticize the president, then you will lose your political privileges," that message was well delivered. But there are several implications. Is digital technology being used to Western Democracy to muzzled free speech?

As men of integrity sit or stand by silently, who will press a finger at the leaking pipeline of information that allows toxic information to seep through with the potential to change the standards created to forge the image of Western man, dear to us? The common thinking that whatever happens in USA will also affect north of the U.S. A's border, Canada. But the thinking does not stop there, it floats around the world. So, the need to apply an optimistic mind set for the benefit of all.

From the fact that these men are knowledgeable in their specific disciplines, so providing rare information to government employees who may not have such experiences, offer significant asset. Surely, taking away access, could further create more chaos in the White House. The flow of freedom of information could also being threatened. Freedom of expression, one of the basic principles leaders of democratic countries are expected to ensure and oversee the practices of everyday situations. This is so, essential, to understand, to enforce.

The expectation to tell the truth as endorsed, under oath is particularly important at law courts in Western countries. To lie under oath can land the witness in prison. During President Trump's Impeachment Trial, a military witness is caught in a trap as his testimony seems to be truthful so no violation against the rule of the courts. But telling the truth portrays The President negatively.

So, two days after the President was exonerated, he fired the witness. Critics claim that the testimony offended the President. Such an action could significantly suggest the need to protect the system from corruption. As innovative technology rapidly delivers information, we see a national response to information. Truth and facts have a variety of levels. Citizens seem to have become "numb" to rapid display of sub-normative behavior as current standardized behavior.

The outcry that a rogue country of the East had injected some form of political, meddling, to generate political disruption in the presidential election generates the possibility of a new form of warfare. Most war is linked with disruption. The disruption caused by cold war that USA experienced in mid-20th Century has minimum disruption on the countries involved.

But the possibility of countries to be using hackers to break into secured **digital** systems put in place to run systems at various government levels violates all the elements of international laws. When countries initiate and successfully implement computer piracy, stealing money from organizations, signals a new form of plundering, digital plundering has evolved.

But outside of meddling, disruption does not stop there, "*posting*" could be used to create disruption. Posting is created on Social Media to generate disruption, to mislead users to create diversion, even to hack into computers of Western countries with the intent to cause disruption, this is Cyber Warfare. Which could potentially take roots in the changing landscape so becoming, an element added to the transforming digital landscape.

U.S.A seems to have the brightest minds when it comes to innovation in digital technology application, yet rogue countries seem able to break in big brand name companies' data bank. Big names carrier like Yahoo.com data bank has been broken into. Although powerful anti-virus software is installed to offer protection against hackers' entry and potentially, yet these viruses seem to find their ways into these powerful **computer systems as these hackers sometimes seem to be one step ahead of their chasers.**

When rogue countries can break into USA firms' accounts and steals millions of dollars then this is a new form of plunder. In days

of exploration explorers take valuables such as gold, silver, wool, and other materials for clothing, from the country being exploited and head back to the European country of origin. Once they are safe in their countries, the goods belong to them and their country.

In modern, digital communication rogue countries or hackers do not have to be in target countries to plunder the resources of that country, in this case to steal their money. They stay in their own country and digitally plunder, the other country, which is break-in the computer system. This is an attempt to display immoral, cyber dominance, to control activities for their own purposes or national objectives.

So, emerging activities, such as breaking into wealthy nation's computer, data base to steal national secrets do have significant implications. Beyond disruptions of manufacturing, military, tech-nology, calls into question the strength of western security to com-bat entry by cyber thieves and hackers working for foreign coun-tries. Some operators of these platforms are managed by owners who are residents of USA skills and innovation of the western world will have to be deployed to offer the feeling of security that western culture consistently represents. Facebook has already established a regulatory group to identify and control rogue countries intended to impact users' accounts because of Cambridge Analytics' issues.

Is it coincidental, that North Korean president, Kim Jung Un sparred with the most powerful leader in the word indicating his readiness to go to war with USA? Social media seems to hype-up, the inter-action between these two leaders. These two strong armed men go back and forth like 2 bad boys in a school yard going at each other. Such an act may not let U.S. A's citizen's experience a bit of unaccustomed fear of entering war on the mainland. But Canadians of the north might have wondered how much of that action would affect them.

President Un gains the respectability to sit down with the U.S.A president to negotiate the possible stoppage of nuclear

built up. Analysts claim that the standard procedure in negotia-tion is to send U.S.A Secretary of State to North Korea to lay the groundwork for the U.S.A President to follow. But since the U.S.A President does not do things the traditional ways and the Digital Era embraces numerous, new ways of doing things, as shown in Digital Tele-communication technology then the time is right to do thing which are not traditional.

But as The President emerged from the negotiation making pleasant remarks about Un while the North Korean president emerged as a recognize nuclear powerbroker being able to turn down the demands of the most powerful leader of the world. The USA president claimed that the North Korean president has given him his words that he has frozen the nuclear build up. As a follow up, for The President, to continue negotiations. Evidence shows that the words of Kim Jung Un meant very little. But his willingness to allow inspectors to examine nuclear bomb testing sites, suggests that such move is a gesture of good will. Even if the president's hope was thrown into the bin, as he had hope to have success where 4 other past U.S.A presidents were not able to.

The tweets seem to be quiet; no news may mean that citizens may have some peace of mind. We in the west like to embrace peace, especially when disruptions are really at our doorsteps. The chaos that was lurking in the shadows promised by President Un,as he boasted that his missiles could easily devastate the coastline of U.S.A mainland. The U.S. President who has been running a chaotic administration, has made significant effort to prevent chaos brought on by nuclear military encounter within the U.S.A landscape.

Business leaders embrace new digital technology that although disrupts the operations of tradition technology used to running busi-ness, such disruption is a positive disruption, efficiency, so meeting short and long terms goals of business.

As disruption seems to be a small component of the digital transforming landscape, **leaderships roles involve making decisions and implementing policies, that generate disruption which eventually, may lead to chaos, that chaos and disruption that may not be noticeable by the citizenry. Not noticeable because of the citizenry trusts in leadership decision making outweighs the generated disruption and chaos. With the minor digital disruption found in the changing landscape, seems to be the doorway for other disruptions.**

Such evidence is seen as the U.S.A President shakes up the friendly organization, United Nation Organization, (U.N.O) causing chaos and disruption. Members of U.N.O share certain commonalities and usually work co-operatively with minimum disruption. Especially when they participate in war, then they are usually functioning as "brothers in arms" and "watch the backs" of one another. The same working expectation is supposed to be followed and implemented by the president but as he addresses the U.N.O representative members at a meeting in France he delivered chaotic, nationalistic tone. The oneness that "brothers in arms" usually expected to signal the continuity of peace and "oneness," was no longer there.

Disruption and surprise were brought in the meeting of U.S.A friendly nations as U.S.A President scolds and embarrasses nation representatives openly.

He reminds them that they are not paying the expected membership fee of being a member of U.N.O. Many world leaders and critics of the president claim that U.S.A should never embarrass its friendly countries representatives, openly but instead, should speak to them privately. The implication, was that the situation of borderline unfriendliness between U.S.A and U.N.O members was created, leading to breakdown relationships between the two, U.N.O and U.S.A.

Emanuel Macron, the president of France, a member country of U.N.O who seems to be a friend of the U.S.A President stunned the global community as he announced at a meeting with his ambassadors that, "Europe can no longer rely on U.S.A for its security". He explained that the current situation of Europe is that Europe security is not strong.

Since the global perception is that USA functions as the flagship of Europe, and for the French president to have held such perception of U.S.A unreliability, suggests that a notable change of perception of the allies of USA. Similar concerns were echoed by the German Chancellor, Angela Merkel response during the United Kingdom withdrawal from the European Union echoes a significant life lasting negative turn of events on the people of Europe. Such changing preception of friendly nations towards one another is reflective of the growing pattern of disruption being at the doorsteps of these nations. We see the potential chaos in the United Kingdom as political leaders fight to manage the consequences of Brexit.

This pattern of chaos fits in with another sampling doing things not the traditional way as evidenced in handling mass migration at some of the USA borders. As information is delivered in real time afforded by digital technology, members of mass migration make decisions to suit their personal outcome. Chaos at the borders fits in with the numerous patterns of disruption in the changing digital landscape.

As these countries operate in a pattern of general disruption, the digital revolution opens to accommodate disruption. For the abundance of information generated by numerous news media create data replacements that deem it not so noticeable and or disruptive. Change will eventually phase out itself as it disappears at *Disappear-ing Horizon of Information.*

The concern was noised about whether U.S.A is still viewed as supportive military power to U.N.O as well as towards other friendly, countries of Europe and Asia. Their fears become real as the president tweets that his policies are focused on making "Americans first". He reinforced his intention when he stamped tariff on certain goods coming to U.S.A from friendly neighboring country, Canada, and showed no mercy on the emerging country Mexico. When he fire-branded China with increased tariff, economists and critics blew the bugle alerting everyone that he had started a trade war, generating fear in business in Canada. These countries, Canada, China, and Mexico, in response placed increased tax on goods coming into their respective countries. Related industries of those countries, slipped into the panic mood, claimed analysts.

There were many concerns in the countries involved. In USA workers in related industries were laid off. Similar issues hit Canada, China, and Mexico. Impacting decisions like the increased tariff, ends up impacting the individual worker. Economists suggested that USA had started a trade war. War leads to chaos.

In early September 2018, Jack Ma, the Chinese business magnate, speaking at a computer conference at Hangzhou said, "Trade friction is unavoidable in technological revolution for China and the USA to grow". He further claimed that friction may last up to 20 years.

Canada and USA historically, have good relationship. But communication between the USA president among other things, seems not at the acceptable level, as the suggestion that Canada is taking advantage of USA may cause our good-mannered Canadians, to ask for those concerned to examine our value system. At the U.N.O meeting at Helsinki, the young vibrant, Canadian Prime Minister, Mr. Justin Trudeau powered out his frustration, as a result of referring to the effects of tariff, as he suggested that Canadians will not be pushed around in reference to tariff the U.S.A president has placed upon lumber and automobile products delivered to U.S.A from Canada.

But silent disruption seems to take another twist, as in summer of 2019, Turkey a member of The United Nations whose military is equipped with USA most updated multi-million-dollar fighter- planes now functioning alongside fighter planes built in the East. The deployed fighter plane, S-400 Missile system operated by Turkey. The "fall out" is that the deployed air defense system would undermine the fighter planes defense systems and is likely to open the functionality of these fighter planes for others to have knowledge of it.

Critics claim that negotiation between U.S.A government and Turkey to use U.N.O missile systems has been in the process for a long time, while Turkey claims that a feasible alternate has not been provided. Members of N.A.T.O are expected to function supportively, but given, the leadership of the USA president who is expected to apply principles of accommodation when dealing with members, instead does the opposite. Therefore, the attitude displayed by Turkey should never be a surprise.

The fast transmission of information by Social Media networks, generated by digital communication is a significant replacement for the slow, former analogue system. This is evident, especially when communication is intended between leaders of countries, when dealing with issues of significance. Such issue of importance, as the Iran Nuclear Deal with U.S.A.

So, when the U.S.A president made his suggestion really happened as he frequently spoke about "tearing-up the USA and Iran Nuclear Agreement," interrupting the relationship between these two countries forged by his predecessor, President Obama, and the leadership of that country. A significant disruption was generated and even if the disruption lays dormant in the thoughts of leadership of both countries, when a new leadership takes over the forging of agreements may take different shapes. A better result could be reached, given the facility offered by digital technology and the many players available to make input in such a deal.

Digital communication provides access of information to varied parts of the world, this very much so within the East. Each varied, political philosophy that drives the cultures of the East as well as the West is responsible for the opposing cultures as much as the east is to the west. Careful attention has always been given when those 2 powerful leaders hold meetings. The press which is supposed to be the mouthpiece that releases information to the public always be present. In the summer of 2018, amid the confusion and disruption that the digital era accommodates, the U.S.A president met with the Russian president with no member of the U.S.A press only a Russian interpreter. This was history in the making.

The result is that the citizens of U.S.A did not know what the meeting was about, information from the meeting, was reported. Speculation was that the president would use social media networks to relay information about his meeting. Such an event has political significance in both countries' history. Up to the end of the year, approximately 6 months later, there has been no reporting on the meeting, as it seems as the data created was swept to the Disappearing Horizon of Information of the West, although likely inactive in the West, the digital footprints left behind by those 2 leaders could be gathering momentum within the networks of the East or West.

Will the West be aware of the digital footprints left for others to view and could use them in the future? Since the technological climate embraces disruption, but luckily for the citizens much of the disruption which could generate fear, innovative technologies are available to eradicate fear. The technologies offer to us hope for the future, along with a feeling of happiness, and great expectation for the future. For much of these bundles of data although may linger in the inactive mindset of the individual, much of it has swept over the

Disappearing Horizon of Information, having little current impact on the individual. But its dormancy does not remove it from the networks, it is still connected, can be accessed by others, to give life in a different form or shape, so impacting others.

From the beginning of the presidency, 75 former intelligence officials have criticized the president on decision making, policies issues. The use of twitter as communication format at a low functioning level, critics claim such practice is not suitable for the level of U.S. A presidency.

The President has made efforts to shut down his critics, this is unusual in a democratic system. Past security advisers play an important role in the security of the country, yet the President takes away their security, access permission.

The President does not view the press as a legitimate instrument of the country as he continued to refer to the press as the enemy of the people. The information the press releases, the President calls "fake news".

Personnel of Federal Bureau of Investigation, (FBI) is usually held at high esteem, as they work hard to protect the USA President as well as to shoulder great responsibility for the safety of the country. Yet he uses Twitter to belittle security personnel who is supposed to provide security for the President as well as security of the country. Such attitude can affect thoughts and attitudes towards the FBI as an institution. Since that is possible, care must be taken, if improvement is needed it must be done in a standardized way.

Change usually evolves into a variety of levels before the acceptable level or standard is reached. Keep that level in mind, the digital revolution has taken the technological culture globally, offering a feeling of comfort than fear. The hope is that the global impact is building up than breaking down, is a perception that drives the feeling of comfort for the upcoming future. The perception of change is gratifying, life improvement for all envisaged in available worthwhile jobs that will lift humans to a higher level of comfort, not much to ask for, to expect, to earn.

The smartness of innovators in recognizing to produce consumers' products or services ties well with purchasing needs of consumers. Such effort encourages consumers to embrace and develop product-loyalty to brand names. As digital revolution affects goods and services, there are indications that the processes in which things are done are likely to be disrupted.

CHAPTER 4

Moving Along the Digital Landscape Using the 3-PointModel

FIGURE 4-1 Efforts deployed to ward off entry to business and organization systems. Shutterstock's infographics.

D igital innovative devices have been so integrated in our life-styles and as the uses increased, so do scammers and cyber pirates seek to exploit users. They also gain entry in users' computer systems and other digital systems to use disruption. As recent technology emerges and are hooked up to the Internet. Cyber pirates find some ways to break in, sometimes the control they imposed is as serious, as imposing a ransom on the user. The pirates then will lock the computer system that they gain access to. This act does not only deny the user entry to his personal system but also shows the level of control exerted over the user.

To repel cyber pirates, the user needs to be fully alert of the preventative methods to be used to prevent access to any access-points scammers and cyber pirates utilize. The safe use of digital information is essential to prevent anyone to use it against the user.

There is a need for the average citizen to have safety-net of protection, as he/she interacts with situations involving a variety digital innovations access point, especially those hooked up to he Internet.

This model may just function as a coping model, for the emerging digital changing landscape. As the digital innovation does not offer 100% preventative solutions to all digital systems. This model may function as just a helpful model that has application for settings such as, at home, at social setting, in consumers' purchasing settings, where personal data is collected in public domain as in a public digital lab. Fortunately, this technological landscape was built on an infrastructure that offers significant stability.

As devices and services are modified and subjected to change, change does usher in fear, along with appreciation and aspiration. As change is recognized as executing technology to improve standard of living, then change is welcome and therefore the need to offer that guidance, is necessary. So, here is a 3-Point Model to help the individual function cautiously in a changing digital landscape. Keep track of new devices on the market, especially those which can be used to invade your privacy. Devices now produce, collect, and send data, be much aware of their presence in your space and what they are actively used for.

3-Point Model

a)Be much aware who is in your social space and what the are doing, especially if the situation offers picture taking. They could be stealing your password of an account you a accessing.

b) Your digital footprints can lead undesirable people to your devices and so right to you. Be careful of how you allow access to your personal information. For those who you least expect may turn-up at your door.

c)We exist in a changing technological world. This technology impact you in all areas of your lifestyles. Educa yourself so that you may participate fully in common area of application such as: at work, at home and in social applications.

Innovative technology ushers in change. So, change is welcome and therefore the need to offer that guidance to users, is necessary. So, here is a 3-Point Model to help the individual function cautiously in a changing digital landscape. Keep track of new devices on the market, especially those which can be used to invade your privacy. Devices now produce, collect, and send data, be much aware of their presence in your space and what they are actively used for.

As the digital technology trickles along the technological land-scape, human lifestyle is impacted. Personal potential is strengthened, a hope to gain monetary value from this modern technology is the ambition of many, as the discovery of new marketable capability of the technology is discovered. This is so evident in the emerging Social Media Platforms.

Large data is a buzz concept for data analytics business, for Social Media platforms as well. Large data creates significant commercial value which means that your personal data when added to accumu-lated data has significant monetary value. Be much aware of those who may be accessing data when you complete any forms that you leave behind with personal inclusive of personal information.

The use of predictive data has become a component used to generate strategic business planning, often focusing on capturing or increasing the firm's presence within the focused market. As the data industry is new, in the near future, the individual also may share in the spoils generated by this new commodity, personal data.

Digital technology has given to human a wearable multipurpose device, the mobile phone, that we have begun to realize that we "can-not do without" has earned the medal for being the top device that has so many services attached to it for access by consumers. There are other devices that offer specific uses when accessed and have sent information, is relatively cheap and easy, so making humans connection likely to be a lifetime adventure.

The efficiency of large storage and fast sending information sys-tems using digital electronic circuitry in these devices are the key to the adoption of these circuits to replacing the old circuits, known as analogue. But as we use these devices in our daily chores, there is a down-side to them. For example, mobile phones built outside of Western countries pose security risk to USA and Canada as suggestion is made that they carry inbuilt components designed for spying purposes. In the same breath, software built specifically to protect users' computers being corrupted by viruses, the same software is reported on as destined to spy on data deployed in that specific computer.

computer. There is much of significant issue arising from the use of 5G technology to be used in Canada and USA.

This technology is developed in Asia is said to have technology that could gather data and send the data back to Asia. But as data has become a commodity to be spied on, so has data has become increasingly abundant, in such a way that such information is beyond our present ability to manage, even significant information gets shove to the ***Disappearing Horizon of Information.***

CHAPTER 5

Disappearing Horizon
of Information

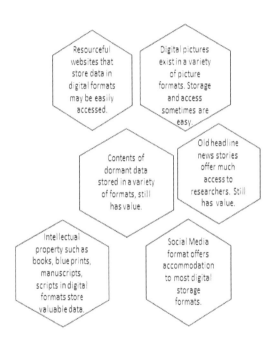

FIGURE 4-2 Infographics showing data in Disappearing Horizon of Information can pose a serious problems.

This is the stage in which digital information seems to disappear from the spotlight. Delivery sources are; Social Media , eletronic tradition media, news stories, video clips books, pictures posted on web sites, any format of digital information is likely to disappear and go dormant at Disappearing Horizon of Information. Information that lies in the data base of any digital devices, equipment, or even any form of data that has the potential to be captured by digital device or equipment for use fall in such group. Such state of dormancy is accessible by others.

This information can be reactivated, as evidence shows that as political personnel intended to enter the 2020 presidential race, and dormant video clips resurrected, revealing information, he/she would like to stay hidden during the campaign of the 45th U.S.A presidency. The worst application brings mystery to a U.S.A super star sent to prison in his old age in 2018 as dormant data has been reactivated and used against him.

Data has value, it is information that commercial firms and individuals would like to access, some legally, others like scammers and cyber pirates, illegally. Personal data talks much about a candidate to be hired, especially when the data seems natural and unpretentious. Hiring personnel of firms, often seek Social Media for unguarded data. They are usually looking for data of the future worker that may reveal characteristic behavior that may not fit in with the culture of the firm, as they go through the processes of hiring such staff members. Often such data may have its origin several years back but although may be out of sight, such data never dies, it just stays dormant awaiting to be reactivated.

So, care should be taken by the individual as he/she interacts within the digital domain, that digital markers left behind do not come back to haunt the individual. When data is accessed in the form of picture, video, or audio, what might have been thought to have never been existed, that data, seems to emerge to haunt the person, to whom it belongs. The warning is, be much aware of those around you with digital devices, is your demeanour able to stand up to scrutiny? With the application of 5G technology, the quality of visual data, such as video clips, pictures, digital video discs, (DVDs) are likely to be high-definition quality. The motivation is therefore, to utilize, the portable devices in areas involving visual and audio uses. Be much aware that the focus is not placed on you. Any picture taken of you is a violation of your personal space and you can demand of that person to erase the picture/s. Here are some essential elements of *Disappearing Horizon of Information.*

Name: Disappearing Horizon of Information.

Location: Cyberspace.

What is it about? Information is stored in variety of formats such as; picture, video, books, magazines, written, audio Social Media posting, websites, etc. see infographic on preceding page. This data may be dormant, but never dies. It can be resurrected and be delivered via the Internet or other communicating formats to be used negatively. Such data may stay waiting for many years to capture the attention of an audience, or to cause havoc to an individual.

There is also data posted on web sites, or as well as postings on Social Media platforms designed to influence behavior. Or spread hatred such data can have negative impact on the individual to whom it is focused on.

Who or what are the suppliers: Social Media, tradition news media, video recording studio, music recording studio, photography studio, publishers of books, magazines, anyone creating data or sends data, especially with the potential to be news worthy or having value, or just from a source as your next door neighbor, taking digital pictures with the potential to deliver the data via the Internet,Chat Room etc. Your personal inform-

ation stored in the data base of personnel offices, business that collects commercial information during business transaction.

(a) Websites, postings on Social Media Platforms, other media formats intended to sway thoughts and standardized conduct. *Those most at risk*:

(b) Social Media users who communicate frequently with other users, using a variety of media formats, as long as they are connected to the Internet, and as long as the Internet exists. Since other users have access to the data in question the potential for the data to be used for other undesirable purposes is there.

(b) Individuals who are at the formative stage of creating standardized acceptable thoughts and behaviors.

(c) Community groups and organizations opened to be influenced by thoughts and behaviors as they follow goals and objectives of their social groups or community groups.

Because data is presented in various formats as discussed earlier, when some or all sites of an organization have deleted your personal data from their data bank, this is usually, a small deletion of what the total is as data may have existed at other locations.

Your personal data could still in existence in data banks of firms, personal computers, social organizations, government agencies, globally, to name a few. The vast area of coverage reflects the expansion of the Disappearing Horizon of Information. The functional capacity of Digital technology does not offer the facility to delete an individual data in formats existing globally, or even to keep track of where it is located.

How it works: Whatever the data is, especially if it gets on the Internet, such data has an everlasting life span. Whenever the data has become inactive, it does not die and goes away, instead it stays dormant in cyberspace, from there, it can be activated. Activation may occur because it has some relevance to a specific person or a headline-issue. Such activation may occur because the data has financial value, and an interested party wants to utilize it.

Global Effects on Data at the DHI: Data that is dormant in Western countries may be newsworthy and have an active audience in other countries. Similarly, such data that is active in other countries for example, countries of Asia, could be dormant in Western countries. This phenomenon is based upon the relevance of the data.

Does Information have to be newsworthy before entry to DHI? Data does not have to lose the attention of an audience to become dormant for entry to DHI. It can go right into dormancy at the Disappearing Horizon of Information. For example, intellectual property not effectively marketed and protected could find itself directly to the disappearing Horizon. Some information in the DHI may enjoy copy right protection, but not dynamic enough to draw big audience attention.

What is the status of personal information at DHI?

Since your personal information could just be in the public domain, care should be taken that whatever is out there, about you, if accessed by others will not have negative effect on you. Information like your bank account number should not be out there for others to access and get into your bank account. Apps designed to signal to the user that he/she has input information that could have

negative effects on him/her, referred to as the ALERT APPS, could create awareness and motivate the individual to take action to reduce access to personal data that could be used to affect him negatively. See chart of alert listing below.

Issue	Possible Consequence	Alert Level	Action to be Taken
Bank a/c no is posted on social media.	Unscrupulous individuals could access you're account.	High,	Alert your bank personnel.
Personal Picture is posted on website or Social Media.	Others could modify it and use it to create false information about the owner.	High	Must act right away by getting picture remove.
Security Software for device is expired.	Hackers, Cyber pirates and hackers could access the system.	High	Renew or purchase security software, have it down loaded to your device.

FIGURE 5-1 Chart showing some issues and consequences of personal data that got left in the Disappearing Horizon of Information.

There are also sites, which focused on objectives that create negative conducts against individuals as well as other communities, such sites may have spotlight shining on them or may not, however, as such sites stay in the DHI, Alert Apps designed to alert the individual of the existence of potential negative impact are necessary.

Information finds its place at the Disappearing Horizon of Information because the information may have lost its current, value. Another newsworthy item or items may have appeared with greater attraction as a result shove that specific news item into dormancy. This initial news item has not been still h as value.

eradicated, its only dormant. Dormancy could occur at a specific geographical location, but the news item could be active somewhere else.

You may even be aware of a news item that should currently re-ported to news audience, but other newsworthy items appear and knock it out of the current listing. The initial news item remains at The Disappearing Horizon of Information. Your personal data that sits in database of numerous firms fits the description of dormancy.

With future application of Artificial Intelligence in household appliances and wearable devices which will be collecting data within their immediate environments, as well as from other devices and equipment pose significant risk. The risk of the individual negatively impacted by data collection right in his private home may require policy in place to offer some form of protection.

Your purpose is to protect your information, in written format, picture format, audio or video. Your personal information does not have to be newsworthy to have negative effect upon you. In making decisions that may affect your personal data, the application of digital model pointer # 3, "What if," especially when you are in doubt.

Here are examples of indication when information is about to slip into the Disappearing Horizon of Information, be hopeful that if yours is there, it is protected or does not pose any significant concern.

Disappearing Horizon of Information

When the featured news item, is faced with at least another compelling newsworthy information that attracts the attention of news audience, so making the initially featured one, less important.

A news story which has been around for a long time that it runs out of steam and, no longer being newsworthy.

An updated version of the news item is available, so making that original news item less relevant. Personal data that lies in the data base of firms that you are a client of. Valued intellectual property in format that can be copied and is accessible, especial at locations where copyrights laws do not apply.

There is personal data accumulated from childhood, moves from school to school with you, seems to have little value but stays dormant. Sometimes when the individual is seeking related data, the record is revisited.

Here are some sources; personal data stored in data base of gov-ernment offices, such as Immigration, Passport Office, Courts Office. Prison records. Records of childhood education, College and University Education records.

WHY DOES THE DISAPPEARING HORIZON OF INFORMATION EXIST?

Any information used in a digital network does not die, it stays dormant. This mean that the information can be reactivated, mod-ified, and used again, creating an image that could embarrass you. Information has impacting effects; it can stay live and can go dormant.

Personal information may carry your digital markers, need protection and carefully analysis of its contents before released in the networks.

Your commercially valid information laying in data bank of firms may appear to be dormant information but can become live when acti-vated. Be much aware of how safe your personal data is.

For the first time in human history the individual is physically connected to thousands of networks in his/her city as well as on other continents.

This means that you:

Can connect by phone, email, Social Media, video clips, through websites, teleconferencing as well as others, connecting with the use of any of the format may access personal information.

Quick transferring of information allows participation in issues occurring in distant land. With the developing and application of 5G Technology, data may deliver 100 times faster than at the present rate. The quality of video clips, pictures are likely to be high-definition quality viewed on your mobile phone. Any of these media formats belonging to you could attract others for social or monetary use. Your place of working hours is no longer limited to your regular workplace. For there are as many firms as possible that allow their workers to work at home, 4 or 5 times per month. So, eliminating the concept that a severe weather day, is a no-work day. The presence of Covid-19 impacts Western countries in such a way that survival of some business demands that employers make changes so allowing workers to work at home.

The human social needs to stay in touch with friends and relatives in distant land are looked after as Digital Technology is instant, faster, cheaper, and often provides instant interaction than tradition methods of communication, others may access your personal data quicker than you think.

As individuals use devices and services Online and off-line, they create digital markers sometimes referred to as footprints. Digital marker offers 2 main uses in the digital technology landscape.

(a) Markers provide a pathway that offers the scope to lead back to you. (b) Your markers can also reveal digital and other personal information about you. Unfortunately, there are those who will cease the opportunity to exploit, steals personal information, act to mislead to rip-off others for their personal gains. You must be much aware of who is around you, and what is the intended behavior. In social set-ting those expected to set socially accepted behavior slipped into social conduct deemed as socially but are sucked into the practice of socially embarrassed behavior that would raise eyebrows if there was a playback of events.

The reality is that the inappropriate behavior when recorded as a simple video clip on a mobile phone the victim is surprised of its existence. These clips usually are embarrassment for the individual often the individual has to deliver some form of explanation relating to his/her social conduct. The eyes of the digital camera are always watching.

So, in social setting, like parties, fund raisers, and banquets, be very much aware of your personal space, what are the digital devices are in active use.

At your home, the need to be careful and be much alert is essential, for there have been scammers pretending to be representatives of institution like the Tax Department, requesting the recipient to give the caller his/her personal social security number. There are scammers calling on your phone pretending, that the phone call recipient is a lottery winner, and to start the money delivery process, the phone call recipient should send some cash to the caller.

Such a call is the initial process to set-up the recipient to steal his / her personal information. Take note of the caller's phone number, hand it to the local police. You may even try to shut him/her down by getting your local telephone service provider to block that number. In that way when the scammer calls back it will not come through to you. If your credit card is actively used at any situations of the social setting or for transaction at commercial check points. Be aware of the safety use of your card, someone peeking over your shoulder could make a note of your password.

In public settings such as checkout counters of stores, a person in the checkout line just behind you, could just peek over your shoulder as you input your password of your debit card. It is also claimed that at some bank machines, hidden cam-cameras are illegally installed to record your credit card number and the password used to access such account, using them for unscrupulous purposes.

The good news is that you can use your digital armor to block access to you. So the basic argument, is emphasis on protecting your personal data, yet there are some who argue and emphasize the need to pursue the application of "open data". The concept of "open data" may be useful in some commercial markets. For example, in publication, expensive data accessible only to a privileged few, if it is made open and accessible to others may have significant application. While medical practitioners in remote areas having access to updated data that digital technology bridges such gap of distance, could use such data in providing medical care for patients would be significant.

As face recognition cameras are deployed in cities for various purposes, personal privacy will become an issue. As consumers' needs arise innovators will produce digital solutions. When both parties are benefited from the exchange, the Exchange theory is at work, the problem still exists to achieve a level of equilibrium in the exchange process. To argue that consumers get their needs satisfied while innovators get their monetary benefits, that is an argument that requires further examination.

CHAPTER 6

Digital Products and Services

1 Some digital devices used in business. Shutterstock images.

FIGURE 6-2 The changing face of Technological Landscape. Shutterstock

Digital technology as it **replaces** the old technology, analogue efficiency achieved. The evidence is present is an improvement in the general standard of living. From the 1970's to present, the emerging digital technology creates new jobs, free up workers as many activities at the workplace are now done by digital technology. As industry responds to digital disruptions, the general effect is that a higher level of efficiency at the workplace is achieved.

As a result there has been a general improvement in life style. It is that kind of efficiency that generates confidence, multi-billion firms such as Facebook, Amazon, specifically, the latter, affirms that initially begins as a book seller, now produces new products, involved in space excursion, researches new digital technology and is responsible for the production of approximately 50 % of USA GP.

The result is that the founder and CEO, Jeff Bezos is on the recent list as among the richest men in the world. Although there were numerous business "starts-up" that allow many young innovators to sell their ideas and start-ups earning within the million dollar range, many were not sustainable and died within a short operational time-span.

This reaction suggests that there is the existing need of planning and running digital technology innovations to generate a last-ing sustainable investment basis, when cyber warlords have the capability to access U.S.A government computer systems as well as private business computer systems to steal secrets, and private data, and able to get away without consequence. This medium is like a digital Robin Hood. Indeed it is rising of a another power-figure. The rising of the cyber warlord. Another trending within the Digital Technology landscape is the ability of Digital Technology to handle large data. Data analytics firms, become important players as they take large chunks of data, making predictive analysis, pre-dicting accurately, focusing on large consumer sales of commercial products to an identified market.

Communication with digital devices in the use mobile phone, use of texting, the portability of the cordless phone offers making and receiving call, at various locations at home is significant in the culture. use of direct speech computer devices, deploying emails. The deployment of digital camera in the mobile phone as well as a device to create images and transfer them for various uses add to the life-changing process.

Development of large firms. Amazon.com which is the largest Online Store and Book Selling company in the world is a product of Digital Technology Era. Big business wields power, the rules though, is that smaller businesses are expected to thrive independent of big business. For small business does have its place in the greater market of a country. Often it is difficult for the operation of the small business to withstand the competition of the big 'goliaths' of business.

A new national conscience is bought to the business platforms. There is evidence that profit maximization is not always the total goal of some business. Big digital business like Microsoft, Amazon, seem to function with a different model, operating with "a heart," so offering new successful business models or modify an existing business model. Such business models are testimony to what this era of digital technology accommodates.

Bill Gates has been generous to charities. His foundation organization functioning in supportive roles to effect changes and modifications of existing practices. This phenomenon could be applied to examine the effects profit distribution has on recipients within profit distribution sector of business. If profit distribution is tried out within the digital technology framework, the significant implications could be observed when practiced.

This could have significant effects on middle income and lower-level income earners. Reflect on the past 15 years on the digital technological changes. Often not much is heard of government regulations. Regulators examined products and services to make sure that what is placed on the market, meet required standards. Although at the same time, they ensure that the vice of control is not too tight that innovators are squeezed out of the market. Within that mix, are household and commercial consumers who have expendable resources, meaning money to purchase these goods and services.

These goods and services are going through lots of changes, as you will understand these inventions cannot be perfected right away. Your purpose in this changing technological era is to;

(A) Use products or services as a consumer at home etc. or a worker at work.

(B) Participate in shaping the product for the general good of everyone. This can be done in supplying feedback on personal use and perception of the products or services. There are some who believe that innovators are usually interested in growth and profit in relationship to their products and services, the formation of community groups, under the umbrella of the specific brand may allow significant access to impact the organization in many areas of development of the product or services. Device like the mobile phone was initially created to make phone call from anywhere, away from home. Now is the world first product that offers so many services connected to it.

An interesting fact is that any of the services offered were in existence before the birth of the cell phone. Currently, the use of digital technology, these services can be adapted and by the application of miniature, digital, microchips circuitry, these services are made available through the mobile phone.

The trend is that goods and services are usually offered to you by manufacturers. But what if you, the consumers have recognized that there is a need common to many people which could be offered through an existing device. The invention of the email makes communication delivery of such to Innovators, C.E.O, Presidents quite to be a possibility from the blue-collar worker to the men at the "top".

In the analogue days, the red tape communication format makes access in communication to people of authority quite a challenge. As often information is delivered through the letter format. This letter when delivered at the venue sometimes, goes from hand to hand and may not even get to the intended personnel on time.

In contrast, digital communication makes direct communication easy via email or social media platforms such as Twitter, Facebook or LinkedIn. Communication is necessary to obtain, improved and analysed information to shape it into the form that you have visualize as well to send it to the recipient who fine-tuned that information into value, be it commercial, social or biological.

It is a fact that you are connected to a network of live Information of countless value. From these sources are available solutions for many. Just think of some common needs of consumers, that researchers would like to monitor on a daily basis. Perhaps the health level of people in a community.

Remember we are in a Digital Transformational Era; the level of societal perfection is not yet reached. Yet innovators have recognized gadgetry attached to arms, fingers, wrist and waist. But the surprise does not stop there, for Santini1 conducted research and secure a patent in USA for microchips implants to delivery drugs in humans.

[2]Basic to this digital drug delivery is the discovery that embryo of frogs can be digitally programmed and possible used to deliver medicine to affected parts of the body. Such finding suggests a significant implication in the delivery of medicine to humans, the possibility of enhancing the quality of life as well as the lifespan of humans in the future is implied in this scientific research.

Available in very much in use are digital gadgetry referred to as Fitness Trackers, there is a wide scope of idea and application" as in the use of monitoring specific areas of our health, or the health condition of our bodies. As innovators recognize and create products to focus on personal fitness. Such business decision is essential

---

[2] Josh, Kriegman, Douglas, Blackiston, Leven, Michael, Team Builds First Living Robot (2020).Vermont, University of Vermont, USA January 13, 2020.

to further identifying other areas and creates essential products is significant.

Fitness trackers serve multiple uses, they produce lots of data, plus analysed data of the user focussing on information of the identified areas of significance such as; stress level, heart rate, body recovery a and age related fitness. Available to relay data on these wearable Fitness Trackers, come in the form of wrist band, and watches. As these wearable devices impact the digital market and find their places in the heart of consumers, innovators may be able to create another level of application of these devices, especially remote component of the technology. In situations where minimum disruption is required, like classrooms, hotel rooms government multi-offices, high-rise and level of application of these wearables could be designed with suitable sensors and actuators to enable security officers and custodians to use wearables to adjust smart heating thermostats to the desired temperature.

Mobile phone has been incorporated in offering high quality supports for health and fitness to the extent that their latest watch carries features focusing on U.S.A Food and Drug Administration, F.D.A approved electrocardiogram (ECG).Along with those features, is the capability to generate pdf with the user's focusing on the related data.

Since the user keep-fit levels are monitored within his/her favorite exercise facility, activities such as; cycling, swimming, jogging, variety of workouts in the gym, even at home when the user is asleep. Such use of these gadgetry is not impinging on the user already limited, available time, but is helping the user to function more efficiently. Our Western culture does demonstrate a keen interest in personal fitness, and if one of the goals is to help the user to be more efficient in monitoring his/her fitness level then there is significant application in f acilitating users to monitor their personal health more closely with the use of digital technology.

There is still much to see, much to examine, much to shape, into that form that generates sustainable existence.

Influencing Elements of Change

Language usage within the Digital Transformational Era is one of the areas that have been greatly influenced by change. New communicating formats give rise to new words and phrases, new beliefs have thrown on the users. As communication has increased in speed, we need to say things quicker, so words and word-phases are shortened. As our voices are the mechanism to draw attention to words and phrases when there is a need to create emphasis, there is minimal problem, when communication format is in written language, the selected word is especially when tweeting or texting, the trend is to capitalize the word of the phrase for emphasis.

But in standard, "Grammar Usage" such usage is a violation of the English Language standards, for standardized "Grammar" is the reference standard for spoken and written language. But even reference standards do undergo changes. Does that mean that we need to update our reference standards as the impacting echo of change vibrates in our reactive mindset and becomes a reality on the visual pages of Social Media? There is much benefit to analyse elements in our western culture that accepts and sustains change as applicable to digital change.

People of power impact change: An example is the current President of United States who uses Twitter to send messages. Gives hints of his taken position on polices headliners. Uses Social Media platform, Twitter to respond to criticism of political issues sending messages to American citizens and suggesting personal opinion as well as decision made on issues.

Global Community and Social Groups: Social groups located globally with shared interest use social media to leverage change so uplifting those who are deprived of personal strength etc.

Celebrities: Celebrities have great followers, their fans who are followers, like to associate themselves with their star. They listen to the celebrities; they will react to their suggestions.

Local Community Groups: Often local community groups evolve because there is a need that affects the local community, as a result a sort of bonding is created to satisfy other needs that demand attention. *Systems* of Existence: Like the Education System, Transport Systems, and Health Systems. The activities within those systems exist to maintain standard as well as to meet the needs of the citizens of the city. The deploying of Digital Technology in operation of activities is an effort to maintain world class standard of these cities.

Critics do suggest that many of these systems functioning styles within these systems reflect traditional practices handed down from generations to generations. In effect little or no diversity is reflected in running of these systems. "Canada, one of the G7 Countries, has recognized the vast impact technological changes are likely to have on its citizenry. In response, the government has made effort to ensure that all citizens are technologically educated as well as able to access necessary quality Internet service. As a result, required digital infrastructure is deployed to accommodate high quality Internet service. Such an initiative suggests the world relevance of technology as well as the high level of preferential focus, placed on digital technology.

To ensure that communities are covered with digital technology, the Federal Government of Canada has created policy to fund initiatives to lay down infrastructure such as reliable WI-FI that facilitates Internet users to carry on with their consumer, commercial, social activities efficiently. The Federal Government earns commendation, as the government has also recognized that seniors of this country, need some help in the changing landscape, in effect funding is given to facilitators to conduct training classes to get seniors

technologically literate, to function in our changing landscape.

There is much evidence that shows the technology is fully embraced. The evidence is at our workplace, city or government departments, recreation facility such as social club or others, some will fully embrace or some may slowly, cautiously moving towards in the usage of digitalization in a variety of applications technology. An organization that relies on feedback from its members to formulate its decision making, may gladly embrace and deploys the use of data generated by Twitter. Guided discussion can be initiated to facilitate projected end-results. Facebook or Instagram, these communicative platforms can pull out much information of significant quality from its members for use to make high quality decision making. A posted message or tweet is deployed to get members reactions. Selected responses could be further analysed and used at a Town Hall discussion meeting format to offer material for use to formulate the main objective of an action plan.

Alternately, don't be surprised if your independent organization does not fully embrace and deployed available digital technology. The old structural model of communication where information consistently flows from the top towards the bottom offers a high level of comfort and control to organization leaders. That form of comfort and control is culturally molded in their mindset. But as digital technology offers easy access of information to individuals, and fashions two-way communication as a channel of making input, many recognize the uses it offers.

Digital communication offers a speaking platform to the voiceless. Leaders must make adjustment of accommodation. That accommodation that embraces the notion that everyone's thoughts and opinions are important must be carefully applied that it is not used in hateful ways. The danger, though as everyone moves to exhibit his\ her personal voice, and sometimes the echo we hear is the echo of hate displayed or an echo to sideline others .

We must remember that our Western culture, which includes to a great degree, freedom of speech also embraces tolerance and respect for others. So as others update their data base, be aware that input contents are free of hate messages. For hate messages have no place to impact other people's thoughts and actions in this media.

Whatever side of the digital culture you are at, endeavor to make rational responses. If there are indicators that you are at the right pathways where your needs and goals are likely to be satisfied, then you are fortunate. If you are at the digital facility that offers limited use of digital services and other facilities that do not meet your personal goals and objectives, then don't be alarmed.

Nothing digitally is completely fixed, plus you are hooked up to thousands of services in your network. This network is a part of; your communities, your cities, your nation, this continent is connected globally. Information is at your fingertips, from Online learning, offered, at colleges and universities. If you are a self-learner, web sites offer relevant information that match your needs. Many seem to think that personal improvement can be done through education. In this case, Online learning could be a way of self-improvement.

Online learning creates a comparative advantage, to driving to campus class half of an hour away. This highlights time as a factor in "among the two". As leaving work to get to classes held on campus is serious factor. Digital technology makes upgrading via online learning, a possibility to many who usually do not have this possibility.

Especially those who live in distance locations, where access to institutions of learning and the ability to pay for expensive courses are challenges. The world Forum1 suggests that e-learning has net worth of $166.5 billion USD while an estimated 25,000 learners globally almost 75% claim that they have taken Online courses. Such data suggests that Online Education is sustainable and offers opportunities for personal development.

Opportunities are available to those whose goals are to earn credits usually offered by institutions of higher education. While if you are interested in taking professional and certification courses to be used to uplift you in your career choice that's opportunity. Most major universities globally offer numerous courses. Then there are fun courses, not intended to offer you any financial rewards, perhaps just to satisfy your higher order needs.

In some areas in the digital technology, perfection and efficiency are not yet attainable. The comparative discussion as to the quality of standards between Online and on-site, campus courses suggest that some improvement is required with Online courses. However, with the emphasis on education for all, there is the effort to establish technological infrastructure necessary to facilitate the use of devices such as mobile phone, laptop and desk top computers. Online learning may be the first stage available to ensure education for all. Which is an indication of the possibility of digitalization has the capability to create a level play-field for all in education goals.

The potential to function as complementary education or alternate education is already made Online learning a favorite. Fortunately, as you are connected to the web of networks, you can search from the comfort of your home. With the use of your computer, you can access your program or your course information on your own time.

Where support information is needed, access to such information is easier as many libraries are now Online, and with many books are now produced with audio copies make access to such information a bit comfortably from home. Where cost and distance, formerly locked you out of your favorite university, now you may even have access. Experimental with virtual campus is something of interest to the adult learner. There is much still in the developmental stage.

Kids who thrive best in homeschooling, kids who cannot be at school during very bad weather, while those who have dropped out of High School without earning their General Education Diploma have needs that can be looked after by the application of digital education. The Education Ministry of Ontario, Canada attempts to make online courses mandatory to high school kids, was rejected. But the disturbance generated by Coronavirus forced the use of Online learning as a viable option. Although it is fair to argue that technology is embraced, yet it may be perceived as disruptive or affects others negatively. Such is the way majority parents of Ontario perceive Online courses for their kids at high school at one time, that perception has changed.

Experimenting with face recognition technology by digital innovators, has application at most border security entrances as well as used to identify potential intruders at private homes as well as at commercial settings. While forerunners firms such as, Amazon's Blue Origin, Virgin Galactic, Orion Span and Boeing, experimenting with space excursion, opens up a new application of digital technology some of which already deployed in industrial use.

AS the digital waves, splash against us and we embrace the change with silent enthusiasm, to those who hold the tools of change whatever is done, be aware that the general good of immediate majority should also an element of priority.

> **The innovator's Purpose in the Digital Landscape.**

The development of a new product is often fascinating, to the innovator and his/her team. The fascination may be associated with the thought of bringing in the bucks, or having your name etched the pages of technology history. Mark Zuckerberg of Facebook, Bill Gates of Microsoft, Elon Musk of Tesla and Jeff Bezos of Amazon not only have their names etched on the pages of history, but their names are on the top listing of the most richest man/woman in the world.

As the innovator delivers the product or service to the purchasing market there is lot of commitment with team members to sell and maintain a consistent clientele for the sales of the product or service sometimes is not an easy "act". For marketing specialist must find new customers. The existence of the worldwide web, with the ease of accessing information and sending information creates potential clients, right at the finger-tip.

The wonder of digital technology to analyse potential customers "Big Data" containing information such as; salary, purchasing habits, demographics allow the innovator to predict, with a high degree of accuracy, customers potential in buying the product or service.

In the consumers purchasing market, in which network marketing prevents innovators from being complacent, for the variety of communication platforms will not allow complacency. Techniques designed to influence consumers are subtle and relatively accurate, as advertisements are tailored to make purchasing impact. Digital shopping offers a variety of options such as; shopping Online, ordering Online and picking-up the product at your selected store, as well as in-store shopping after viewing products Online. Even drones are experimented with 'drop-off 'items delivered to customers' homes. Over the past 5 years there has been a significant growth in Online shopping. In 2018 reports show that Online shopping has grown to $3 billion U.S.D. If the market is so vibrant no wonder stakeholders execute strategies to arrest consumers purchasing attention.

It was evident in 2015, the Canadian technology firm, Blackberry supplied about the greater portion of the Canadian and American business, phone market with the Blackberry mobile phone. The 44th president, Barack Obama used that kind of phone for his business work while 'in office'. But by the end of 2016, the technology giant of Canada had lost the greater portion of the market to the two rival firms, Apple and Samsung located outside of Canada.

To maintain the share of the market, to obtain new customers and retain existing customers' loyalty, some firms used dominant techniques that sway other customers towards them. Some digital venture excels and expand while others close their doors the phenomenon of change and adapt to the digital landscape affects some positively while others negatively. Change and disruption may appear to be so intense that entrepreneurs may have to deploy the strategy of, "survival of the fittest". For this digital landscape is new environment of digital ecosystems in which players maximize the uses of existing resources to survive and excel while some give in and so perish.

That may be so, as new technology comes into existence and is deployed, innovators who can utilized the relevant technology in their business may survive as well as etched their name on the pages of history. As innovators execute business strategies, they may appear to take on a negative image. Could the outcome is really the result of "survival of the fittest" in a changing competitive market? After all, Bill Gates gives away millions of dollars to charity. When Amazon builds a distribution venue in native communities, in Canada, such acts seem to be a moral decision and offers a path for many not only to think about but to activate the element of engaging.

It may seem that consumers stand helpless under the influence of power of innovators. Over the past 5 years there has been evidence that computer software, laptops and desk top computers have been reproduced for the market without any significant added features. Yet consumers seem to have been influenced to believe that they need the new products although the original product that they have seem to be functioning well. Innovators could argue that since their business need to survive, therefore, strategies used are survival techniques are relevant.

So, the fine line between influencing consumers purchasing habits and executing survival techniques for business is perception decision. The application of the concept of an educated consumer is the best customer, should be embraced by you, the consumer for the Western society that we live in everyone is a consumer.

CHAPTER 7

❦

Internet an Accelerator of Digital Transformation

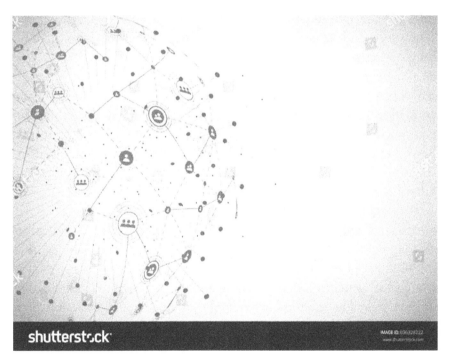

FIGURE 7-1 Internet, a connection of networks transcending geographical borders. Shutterstock infographics.

As new product or service emerges in the market, the firm that manufactures that product or offers that service, the basic goal is to remain in operation. To sustain the existence of such product or service of the emerging technology, dependency is rested on consumers' purchasing attitudes. So, the firm must influence the purchasing attitude of consumers so that they buy these products and services. The firm then has deployed skilful techniques in impacting consumers purchasing attitude.

Available personal data in great quantities function to signify to the investor that here lies resources that is increasingly becoming a commodity. So as many emerging firms use "Big Data" analysing it, with high level of accuracy, gives new use and value setting the stage for continuous future applications of personal data. As data has a new use and value, so does your personal data become an item sought after for unethical use by others.

Data in picture format seems to be targeted by some. By using animation procedures, an individual's face can be doctored, voice can be copied showing a verbal and physical action done but in reality, never happened. But the good news is that there are emerging firms ready to offer protection, to stop scammers whose intention is to use others' identity for unethical purposes.

Search engine such as Google is designed to personalized information, so claimed Eli Pariser in his book, "The Filter Bubble," that in 2009, era of personalization had begun. Some media giants use the strategy of "watching what you are searching" and so provide links that interest you. The main objective is the more personally relevant than information available, the more advertisement these media platforms can throw at you, the more minds are awakened.

I search a specific site for a cover casing for my tablet, making no commitment, just checking out the prices and styles. Two days later that specific site sent me an advertisement with 4 casings at discounted prices. No doubt, this Internet giant, watches your purchasing

purchasing habits as well, analyses your data, identifying related, relevant information that has commercial value that site and its affiliates, and so harvests your personal data for commercial use. But such practice is an indication of the Exchange Theory being put to use. The customer is offered the opportunity to shop for the best possible deals while the seller's products are bought out of the store.

Search engines and media platforms attract over 100 million users who send texts and write blogs daily. During such processes, information such as age, salary, geographical location, needed products, services are being searched for. Such large amount of data for firms is essential for efficient operation of the firm. If consumers purchasing attitudes show that consumers within a certain city tend to buy computer laptops than desktops, then it is business sense to sell to consumers in that city, laptops than desktops.

Similarly, if analysed, consumers data showed that parents are moving towards purchasing electronic toys than non-electronic toys the manufacturers are likely to market electronic toys to parents and kids. But advertisements are not only designed to bring to the attention of consumers with the products and services needed for sale. They are designed to impact our thoughts and purchasing attitudes.

We may want to think that the more information we get the better and more independent consumers will be. It is contrary to that thinking, as Eli Pariser suggests the trending is to set us up for a "custom tailored world". We sometimes buy consumer products in "packaging" but in our digital transformational world "packaging" is placed with the emerging buzz word, "custom tailored".

Since digital systems used to produce products and services, tend to generate a higher level of efficiency. Comparatively, "custom tailored" products are focused on the group concept. As the technology landscape changes, we see a shift, focusing on specific mass design and production of products based upon analysed factors.

So, our personal information has discovered to have value. "Information value", is comparable to the early evolution of labour in our society. That is another emerging phenomenon of the digital era. If we reflect on the caveman period where labour had almost zero monetary value. But labor had significant "field and household" value as well as group security. In terms of community security. As we moved from the agricultural economy towards the industrial economy the commercialization of labour takes on much value. We are at the initial stage where individual personal information worth million of dollars when used in great numbers. From the fact that when personal data has great value in big quantity. It is quite possible that personal data evaluated in some commercial way that it has monetary value for the individual.

Some factors that determine grades of value could be focussed on some commercial elements such as; (1) Yearly income. The greater the salary of the individual, the greater the purchasing power of the individual. (2) Professional title. Owners of certain job titles do not only have status but makes a statement of employment stability. (3) Communities' Specialization Factors; such as farming communities in comparison to a city with much commercial activities, peaceful communities in contrast to war torn communities. (4) Medical condition of a person's health. Medical health may impact purchasing attitudes of the individual. (5) The level of debt of the individual. An individual with little debt may have greater purchasing power than others who are in financial debt.

Focused groups working along with governmental agencies could make significant input in shaping the outcome. Will those components that offer significant, social value to individuals prior to the digital era can be transformed to monetary value, is yet to see?

Brand name of an individual or a firm, is a buzz word for young entrepreneurs. The focus placed upon the market value of "brand" and what seems to create the value of the brand varies from brand to brand. What is evident is how the market reacts to it. There are some discussions on creating access to what is referred to as "Open Data". As

Smart Cities begin to evolve, outside labs are proposed to be built in the city of Toronto, Canada but has been struck down may be the community is not ready to accommodate such level of openness outside labs would offer.

The many new digital devices and some established equipment, now connected to the Internet produced data and or collect data, in this digital era. Consumers in this marketplace has multi-function, they not only offer monetary resources upon purchase of the product or service but also offered well valued data in the process. This is evident in the use of commercial apps, wearable hand and wrist bands which collect and store data to be harvested later. Quite likely commercial apps function to track the user, collecting data on his activities at various places of visits. The value of mass data is too significant to by-pass, innovators seem to jump on the "bandwagon" of third valued resource of the individual in a highly digitalized countries like Canada and USA. So, the Digital Era is remaking the individual into a *tri-ple-resource supplier.*

At the work place it is a well-established fact that the workplace depends on the labour of the individual to produce products and services. This practice is a normative expectation in Western society. The new expectation is that the individual is a supplier of data. He is not helpless, for he embraces the prediction of computer analysis offers that as digitalization increases in all areas of industry and our lifestyles, the individual will enjoy a higher quality of life. He does not need to escape from society as Fromm claims in his book, *"Escape From Freedom,"* for he loves the digital make-over. As he now realizes that he cannot do without his digital mobile phone. Like a thirsty man is drawn to water to quench his thirst he realizes that he is drawn to the use of his digital device, his mobile phone to maintain his digital destiny of global connection.

If innovators continue to function on the principle of profit maximization, then personal data could be in danger. For the drive to utilize data will likely to be a part of the decision making processes, unless innovators who have demonstrated reasonably decision of looking out for the interest of the average consumer may influence others to participate in demonstrating in protecting the interest of the greater majority, in this case, personal privacy.

In a vibrant economy like our Western culture, commercial activities take shape rapidly. There are numerous analytic firms have developed, the main purpose is to analyse "big data for commercial uses. In comparison of gathering information by using the old surveying method, data analytic lets the old surveying method looks like the difference between day and night. The application of data analysis in other areas apart from business is slowly emerging.

When the Canadian Federal Government has funded a data ana-lytic firm that is using data to prevent mis-demeanour from happening to individuals that social workers and counselors would have to rem-edy such problems, is an indication of application of data analytic use in other areas. As a matter of facts, analysed data has found its upscale use in so many areas of industries that it may just be that moment of readiness is waiting for someone to unlock and individualize the value of personal information.

Information re interconnected and available, analysed data could play significant role in maintaining efficiency in all areas of inter-connected departments. The task is to deploy the change-over without slowing down the efficiency of the others, when circuity has to be deployed or machine parts modified.

As for compensation, to individual whose data is used,the best possible scenario,is embedded in the Exchange Theory as used by SocialMedia. Valuation of individual data based upon the award seems to carry insignificant commercial value to the individual, but media platforms which have access to data of billion of users, the commercial value is in the millions of dollars, USD but as clients are offered free use of these services, then it appears that both party benefit from the exchange process although it may appear that the level of benefit for each party has little comparison.

The current trending is commercialized the value of personal data focusing on great quantity. This option may provide a miniature benefit for the individual consumer. Data analysis has its application in so many areas that are necessary to take a close-up examination of data analysis.

The quiet changes of our technological landscape could not be better for our Western culture, the emerging technology has been embraced and integrated in traditional industries. New devices have become a part of our daily cultural use, a visible technological imagery of western culture has started to take shape in the form of wearable digital devices.

Wearable devices such as; keep fit wearables are worn on the arm, wrist and finger. Headphone sets that interfaces with the mobile phone is worn on the head while the mobile phone which has become a record breaking device with so many integrated uses, are placed in pockets, bags, attached to waist belts and even in pockets of the shoulder.

A human need, such as the need to socialize, gives rise to the origin of Social Media, to facilitate interaction and communication with friends, meeting and making new friends, all have been embraced with open arms by people who are involved. As the individual uses digital devices, much data is generated, stored as well as passes onto other data bases. These data bases have commercial value information to data analytic firms. So, the average user our western culture is globally connected to thousand of goods and services providers all over the world.

Though it may seem that the existing emerging technology that is impacting humans in our technological landscape, is largely

determined by 3 main commercial purposes fashioned by the Industrial Revolution.

These concepts are; (1) Each adult individual has the potential to be a consumer. Therefore, will buy goods and services that are on the market. (2) Each adult individual has the potential to work. Therefore, so will contribute her/his skills, to the workforce , and is ready to participate in the manufacturing and sales of products or services.

But slowly in the emerging stage, although having significant commercial value to the industry, but no monetary value to the individual who owns it, this is personal "data." So, this digital era has transformed you the individual to; (3) A supplier of personal data. Education institution, enrollment at social clubs, are samples where your personal information is passed on to these organiza-tions and institutions. where it goes into their data base for use at their will.

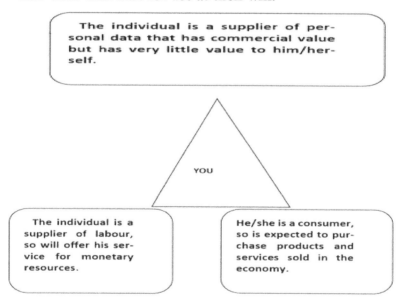

Figure 7-2 The Commercial Value of the Individual within Western Culture.

The Individual has 3 elements of a commercial profile in our Digital Landscape.

As focused groups evolved and take up their responsibility to advocate for themselves and others by participating in shaping the destiny of what our new technology landscape will be in the future. As there is always be the need of someone or a group to be the voice for the general good of the majority, such role can make significant input.

As such emerging commercial activities impact you, you the citizenry has a participatory, engaging role. It may just be to find a niche within these emerging commercial activities, seeking the appropriate tools and utilizing the skills and support of innovators, law makers, social workers, men of conscience and men with great vision to create focused groups to deal with these emerging commercial activities on behalf of each individual. To charter pathways that such technology landscape will take in the future.

Many of the systems that run our society today have their origins from the days of exploration and discovery, we are now in an era where changes are occurring that will lay the foundation of what the "is of things" will be perhaps up to hundreds of years, if you have the drive and the skills you may just have your chance to do something good for humanity.

It is also gratifying as some innovators have made it big in the area of digital innovation, and have amassed a fortune, even seem to give back to communities significantly. They may be laying the ground works for modification of The Exchange Theory.

This principle that seems to have that great force that drives the conduct of firms and in this case innovators. It is that principle that suggests that the firm or innovator go into business to maximize their profits. Since some innovators donated great sums to charities and community organizations, they may just have begun to shine the light to bring to the attention of others that personal monetary need maximization embedded in the principle of profit maximization, can be subjected to modification as practiced by some digital innovators, specifically in USA.

So, the question is why should you the individual be involved in such a task? The response is that an examination of *a scientific law of motion* will explain the evolution of such natural response of the individual in our changing technological landscape. *This law of motion suggests that for every action there is an equal and opposite reaction.* In this context, emerging technological devices and services that impact the individual represent "actions".

Now take a close look at the numerous technological devices and services that the individual has to purchase, learn to operate them, has to get the money to purchase them to use and remember passwords to stop intruders from entering his/ her private domain. These are just some of them; mobile phone, laptop and desktop computers, digital watches, wearable keep fit monitors, the tapping credit cards.

The evolution of new platforms fired by; Social Media giants; Facebook, Instagram, LinkedIn, WhatsApp bring to the individual a new line of digital products for business and household communication. We embrace them with much expectation for texting, email that the average person has to bring in his/ her lifestyle are immediate changes. Posting on Social Media, creating and sending video clips, and send picture formats are just great for those who want to socialize.

The use of GPS service on the mobile phone and other devices as compass to guide the motorist in and round town These digital responses that the individual has to react to, are comparable to the concept of "actions." Such actions responses from the other individual caught up in the behaviour. So, the opposite of "reactive responds" is "proactive responsive".

Those caught up in the digital framework are usually displaying proactive responses to digital cues within the digital landscape. When individuals love and appreciate elements that generate responses they embrace and protect these elements and will even utilize the elements to maximize the highest outcome. This is what happens to Digital Technology.

Basically, there are 3 basic stakeholders working supportively in shaping the digital landscape.

(1) You, the individual representing yourself as well as the general good of the people .

(2) The Innovators and the firm.

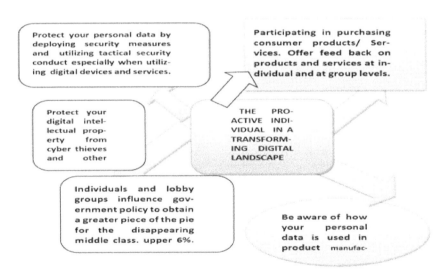

Fig 7-3 The individual participation in shaping the emerging Digital Technological landscape.

(3) Government policy and the consumer utilizing their purchasing power.

The free market in our Western society offers the scope to innovators, to conduct research to discover and develop new products and
services. Economists, usually argue that consumers demand for such
products and services should determine the course and life sustainability of each product and service. As consumers usually functioning in
a reactionary mood and sometimes seem helpless, government estab-
lishes regulations to protect consumers.

Government roles not only for protection, but participate in areas
such as funding for research and product development. The offering
of protection to rights of ownership of products, impose punishment
on those who break copyright laws without the owner's permission
on a global level. To enforce intellectual property rights globally, to
encourage firms to collect incentives that by convention belong to
them. Below is a model that explains the role of Government regulations impacting the digital landscape.

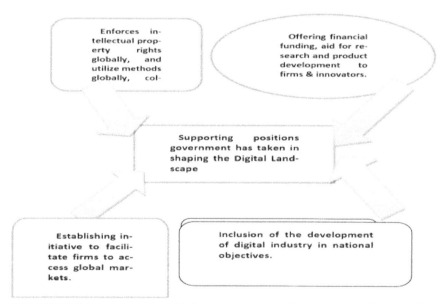

**FIGURE 7-4 Some areas in which government regulators impact the emerging
Digital Industry**

When government understands the significant impact that technology can have on a nation then makes commitment to support the digital industry, is quite likely to encourage participation many areas of the industry.

But the reactionary mode that the individual has found himself/ herself is not a phenomenon of the rise of Digital Technology but has been reinforced by the Industrial Revolution and further utilized in the digital era. For as innovators and firms seek to sustain their business and sell their products and services, they seem to feel that they are to use available tools and strategies to ensure their objectives are met. The Internet is the major phenomenon that has impacted and transformed the technological landscape as has never been seen before.

This Internet has broken down the privacy door which has offered to some degree, a level of privacy and security to the individual. It further has tied the individual to networks of products and services so forcing the individuals to create digital footprints which can lead intruders to the individual's personal privacy. Although these issues seem to have created by the emergence of the Internet, a negative image seems to have forged linking the Internet to it. There is much benefit derived from the Internet. It is viewed as one of the significant technologies which functions as the lifeline of Digital Technology responsible for changing the technology landscape, locally, nationally, and globally.

Firms are emerging to partner with, other firms, government agencies, innovators, and consumers set to create new services and products. With the intent to convert analogue equipment to digital, new dimension of services and efficiency in business operations are developing. Equipment collects data and communicates with other equipment and devices. Efficiency is sought as machines is programmed to think as humans. Comparative efficiency is always an issue, as it is believed that the human's brain will always have a higher level of efficiency, the future holds the truth.

In turn the individual uses the Internet to interact, with friends, relatives, and do personal business. In the process, he/ she buys products and services. Messages are sent via email and texts, releases information via video clips and picture formats, re-ceiving and sending messages via mobile phone are some of the digital responses that generate digital foot prints. As you may know, footprints in the snow or soft soil can be traced back to the person who has made them.

Because you no longer have a privacy entrance door as the Internet has destroyed your privacy entrance door, you are opened to anyone roaming the Internet. There is hope, for the Internet lockout door, the "password,"along with the use of anti-virus software to prevent viruses to damage your computer systems and careful protective use personal information. Sensitive information such as phone number, account and bank identity numbers, even the release of personal wealth information, could generate negative response towards the individual.

Just as you have a moral responsibility to pay your taxes, to obey the laws of your country, you are also expected to participate in events or issues relating to the general good of the country. The emerging image of the technological transforming individual is not only to react to the objectives of business activities as related to digital sales and manufacturing of devices, but to be a proactive participant in the direction that digital landscape is changing .

The preceding 2 commercial purposes of the individual are commercially/ consumer driven based upon business digital activities. While the third purpose is moral obligation driven. Based upon the newness of so many digital innovations, there is possibility for these technologies to drift in unchartered direction. But since our culture still embraces the concept that everyone is expected to act for the general good for the society, then the individual as a stakeholder can act for himself/ herself and for the general good of the country.

This, is to utilize the resources that Digital Technology offers such as communication platforms that transfer large information quickly and easily made by communication formats such as email and text. Issue based existing, community proactive groups do have a role to play in discussing of issues related to products. So many manufacturers welcome feedback, information to be used to increase company's/customers goals.

On a global basis, activists have used Social Media to create issue-based groups and educate women as to their human rights etc. Similarly, community groups, wanting to control hate and immorally in-appropriate postings, use the platform to educate potential victims.

Lawmakers enact laws to maintain desired standard, constituent members bring firsthand information to lawmaking process. The fast relaying of information which is one of the key elements of digital technology when used by constituent members associated with focused groups seems to strengthen their base and offer a sense of solidarity.

There are some firms that welcome focused groups members' that will enlist feedback on their service/product. Having to talk to the company representative may generate significant benefits on both sides. There may be a representative that is available for communication purposes. Connect with him/ her if possible. Many firms are happy to get feedback from firsthand users of their products or services. Community groups, national 'focused groups' are helpful resources for shaping the direction digital technology will go.

Experts claim that data analysis is the use of large amount of data to be analysed with the objective to discover generated patterns and using those patterns to predict relatively accurate likely, future events. This is exemplified as analysed data used likely, future events. This is exemplified as analysed data used market products based upon consumers purchasing attitudes of particular products. Data analysis is categorized in 3 main grouups.

Descriptive Analytics: which is the effort to use in reference to "big data" to describe events.

Predictive Analytics: which is the effort to use "big data" to predict events or generate responses.

Prescriptive Analytics: which is to create solutions or generate responses for issues at hand. Data analysis has found upscale use in many industries, and software used to analyse data are so accurate that industries such as; Colleges and Universities, the Manufacturing Industry, Healthcare and Telecommunication, just to name a few used data analyses to ensure performance efficiency.

In a world where commercial activities impact our image and as shown in our in what we wear, eat, and how we socialize. It is essential that the individual does not only take an reactive position to all these events that impact him/her but utilize a proactive role in meeting these activities face to face. So, if goods and services are tailored to meet the purchasing needs of consumers dictated by predictive data analysis, rational reactions should be the responses to the analysis of the rational reactions[3]. So, that the consumers intended goals are achieved. If the goal is to obtain 'goods and services to be 'tailored' to meet the purchasing needs of consumers' responses, then that is done. The impact of the Innovator with the firm on the technological landscape is one of our great world events in modern times.

---

[3] A rational response is generated when the individual analyses the situation then makes the best possible decision.

FIGURE 7-2 Infographic showing The Innovator's impact on Digital Technology shaping the nation.

Soon, in the future consumers will be fashioned to respond to tailored goods and services that they like. When goods and services are tailored for people, then choices are limited. Freedom of choices is a basic principle that many in West and Eastern culture cherish and embrace.

But tailored products are not really new, as our society becomes more commercialized, goods are packaged, according to pricing, spacing, weather condition and others. Critics seem to believe that Digital Era offers opportunities to guide consumers attention to accept commercially tailored products. As individuals use their devices on the Internet, commercially, focusing on products tailored to the individual needs, these products are flashed in the faces of consumers. The intent is to influence the consumer purchasing attitude. Social media giants make use data and demographic characteristics such as age, the location of users. The gender of users as   well as social interests are among the characteristics required analysis.

But as data is being analysed there are hackers and scammers who are planning to access your personal data of individuals. Related data; such as credit card account number, bank account number, as well as information related to access such accounts. Protection of individual personal identify is high on the security level. Just to create havoc with the individual's personal lifestyle. For the privacy door is no longer a barrier to intruders or unwelcome guests. In our innovative culture when there is a problem, solutions are usually being sought, such practice is usually for the general good of the people. The benefits usually shared by the innovator and as well as the firm.

Treatment and prevention of illnesses depend much on lengthy gathering of data. Time consumption is partly due to examining the data, looking for patterns to make medical decisions. Innovators must cease the opportunity to identify areas in medicine in which data analysis has much use in the treatment and prevention of illness.

It is those pathways that previously, the individual has to walk, through historic university entrances, paying big bucks to access classes where students of distinction sit. Websites of personal issues to the individual can be accessed from the comfort of your personal computer in your living room. While revealing the meanings of concepts, phrases as well as single words, is a reflection of the data persons agility to utilize digital devices to access informative of related data base.

We must remember that there are those out there bent to make havoc with the others personal lifestyle. For the account number, as well as information related to an individual personal identity privacy door is no longer a barrier to intruders or unwelcome guests. In our innovative culture when there is a problem, solutions are usually being sought, such practice is usually for the general good of the citizenry. The benefits usually go to the innovator and the firm.

CHAPTER 8

A NATION OF PEOPLE
WITH NEW DIGITAL
PROFILE

The **internet that breaks down** your privacy entrance door, has so many services connected to it that as you use it unavoidably fallen in love with it. Therefore, earns recognition of examination of what the Internet is all about, as the individual uses it, how he/she can protect himself/herself. The Internet in its simplest form is like a network of roadways existing in space. This network allows digital devises to send and receive data to individuals and business near far away in terms of thousand of miles away while as near as your next door neighbor. The average person in our technology landscape understands the Internet and maximizes the various uses of the Internet.

The Internet is not the first medium that forces entry to our pri-vate home. The line phone has been doing this for a long time, so does radio as well as television signals. They function on a one-way communication principle, excepting the line phone which adds a reactive mood so may facilitate two way communications, so facilitating a direct feed back to the sender at the other end.

The contrast with the Internet, is that it is not a device, but a part of an invisible network of road ways that exist in the atmosphere, that facilitate others using their digital devices, to send and receive data along the network of roadways even in the privacy of their homes. That is why when your son or daughter is doing his/her homework using the computer or tablet, you need to monitor who he/she is communicating with. For someone, thousand of miles away could be sending inappropriate messages using such devices such as; mobile phone, laptop desk top computers or tablets. The rise of the Social Media platforms such as Facebook, Twitter, Instagram etc. are designed to generate a reactive response as the individual signs-up for what appears to be a relatively low-cost account.

Learning the routine is a simple process. The new user observes what others are doing, and she/he reacts by imitating them, your friend posts personal picture for others to see so you post yours too. When friends make eye catching comments, on an incident or others comments on other posting, then you react by making your posting or comments too.

The ease of sending video clips and digital pictures over the networks to add "color" or legitimacy to a news story, even to advertise a product is evident. In 2016-2017, countries were concerned that rogue countries would break in their data base and steal their secrets relating to their manufacturing and scientific research. Cyber attackers were the concern of those roaming the Internet looking for any weakness in the system to commit havoc. Cyber attackers do not only break into the data base of the governments of the Canada and USA but also accessing data base of private business, as well. Internet providers struggle a lot to prevent cyber attackers from, stealing million of dollars from customers' private information.

Rarely is the practice of private information of the individual locked away in metal cabinets at the office. The emerging digital technology now offers storage in accessible digital sites, as well as desk top and laptops and portable storage data sticks via the Internet as well as databases of business computers. This "Big Data" in data bases of firms entices cyber pirates to break in business computers, gov-ernment computers networks, personal computers all kind of digital devices that stores data.

If there were no internet, it is safe to say that there would be no Social Media platforms in operation and function as they are today. As The Internet provides the pathways back and forth from user to users they communicate with one another, the value of the new platforms and variety of uses become evident to entrepreneur. Individual such as Justin Bieber, owes the launching of his career to the internet and the social media. Meanwhile, market experts of firms recognize the great number of potential customers, by contact, they seize new marketing strategies, such as the" customizing model", and the intense use of data analysis, plus the emerging platform refers to as Digital Marketing.

The mind is curious, so individuals wants to examine the new packaging of consumer products sold under the title as tailored goods. But if curiosity is the inward motivator that drives the consumer to examine the product, then a great part of the marketing strategy is done. It is up to the expert to make the consumer being hooked onto whatever is being marketed. Some products and services will go on forever, some will not.

The desire of the marketing experts is to influence the purchas-ing appetite of the consumer that he/she devours the product/service with such intensity, on and on so that they become sustainable, always wanted by the consumers. From the fact that there are billions of users of the Social Media, suggests that the rise of Social Media has come into effect the right time to fill the social needs, which industrial psychologists refer to as one of the mid-order hierarchical needs.

With such great number of users attached to Social Media, a common trending, which is similar to the mobile phone has begun to emerge, multi-servieces. We are quite aware that there is no other device ever invented that offers so many services as the mobile phone. Does current trending parallel the mobile phone? Or is it that the digital phenomenon is fashioned to link multi-services to one device, e.g., the mobile phone?

Social Media platforms, not a device but a service platform offers more than one services. It is used to encourage users to socialize with one another. Social Media platform is emerging into one of the most comprehensive medium to market goods and services via the Internet. It is also used to place value on users' personal data and when placed in great number, "Big Data" the prized, product is transferred along the Internet, the value is in billions of dollars. Such worth and value are evidenced in Technology cities such as Silicon Valley, Toronto Canada, Seattle and New York City, just to name a few.

New York Times suggests at the end of 2018 that personal data is the most prized commodity in the Digital Era. Facebook with its users amounting to 2.2 billion users generate access to "big data". Facebook offers "a voice to the voiceless", claims the CEO, Mark Zuckerberg. If this is so, as people are connected, talking and listening to one another changes may take place. Maybe the evidence is seen as global response to police excessive force and killing of young Blacks in U.S.A. The provision of relatively easy access to these Social Media accounts help participation in the cause.

Could media along with the Internet be the medium to effect social changes such as community participation in laying down basic infrastructure, participate in regulating digital uses of devices and services? The possibility is endless.

As Digital Technology brings along with it access to information. Information empowered people, especially those who have been suppressed by leadership unwilling to share power. Leadership is confronted to make changes, especially put into practice procedures that will offer access to decision making access. Traditional, leadership can begin by open to dialogue on changes in accommodating those left out of making input in decision making. Leadership may begin by accommodating input, by all. The accommodation and utilization of progressive business principle that embraces the fact, that an individual participation in an organization is enhance when he/she shares in the decision-making process.

The limitation of quantity of words that Twitter, format tends to accommodate, may be a blessing in disguise. In contrast, to new stories of newspapers and magazines carrying 3 or 4 paragraphs makes twitter looks bad. For only a small fraction of such is permissible.

Twitter offers opportunity to state the message short wording and up to the point. As thousands or millions of viewers may cast their eyes at the communicated item. That limited space has no offer for a developing news story. Neither is present to guide the 'freshman', "standards and procedure". While Social Media offers to the individual a voice of his/her own, *The Internet offers to the individual, pathways to access an unlimited world of data.* This new path seeks to make the 'playfield' a little more level for both parties.

Websites with information needed by the individual can be accessed from the comfort of his/her personal computer at the liv-ing room. Fast search engines allow the user to access, ideas, his-torical dates, geographical locations, prices of items, you name it search engines will take the user there in seconds only within a time frame of 1 or 2 minutes.

The average user is like being at an upgrading class once you have access to your device attached to the Internet. *Western man no longer has to sit at the feet of great men to be a learned man.*

He now seeks information by himself from the thoughts of wise men, the data base of great universities and from the links and sites of powerful organizations.

But as data is being accessed for healthy uses so are hackers and scammers planning to access users' personal data. To play havoc

with users' personal lifestyles. In response to protect Canadian digital technology users, a call alerting technology designed in alerting the local phone call could be a possible scammer.

This is in response to a directive from the Regulatory Tele-communicating Government Agency Canada Revenue[4] reported that scammers robbed $16.7 million Canadian dollars from local citizens. They posed as officials of Government department, chiefly products/services of Associated with western culture are elements of certain visual imagery that mirrored him/her as an individual of Western culture. Examplified are jeans clothing, as used in pants and jackets.

Associated with Western culture are elements of certain visual imagery that mirrored him/her as an individual of Western culture. Examples are, jeans clothing, very popular as informal wears. The comfortable canvass 'shoe-runners' are other visual imagery of western culture. Timely, Western individual is taking on a digital image and profile.

Users of Social Media love the Social Media communicative platforms. The media giant, Facebook has over 2.2 billion users in digital, global, landscape. This suggests that giant consumers' market the innovative technologies have created for sellers/ buyers, in variety of commodities. or brand loyal has driven users to take on an adaptable life style common to the Social Media. products that change the visual digital imagery globally.

Since the existence of Western society is partially because Western man is fashioned to exercise purchasing attitudes. This attitude offers the first steps innovators need to understand consumers attitudes towards products and services.

[4] Canada Revenue Agency

It is a known fact that The Internet is a significant facilitator, to move digital commodities from local markets to national and global markets, this phenomenon helps to offer sustainability to the commodity. That sustainability is essential for manufacturers. As digital commodities become increasingly a part of the national culture, as well as leading paths towards integrating global culture with Western culture, that may be a sign that the digital commodity is emerging as a part of visual digital imagery of Western individual.

There are some potential emerging, products on the market that could *become a part of the visual imagery,* not necessarily in the existing format or the existing featured services presently offered. But in the form that will attract the attention and purchasing needs of individuals.

Products such as wearable, keep fit monitors just could be the potential products. Western individuals like to be much aware of their health conditions. The visibility of the mobile phone is seen during its use, carrying cases are designed for most brand names of mobile phones but seem sometimes have been placed in pockets or handbags. This could be a spin-off product of Social Media, be a visual that causes the individual to embrace it with much enthusiasm? Facebook generates a spin-off, Dating a sort of dating platform. Social needs alway placed high on the preferential needs pyramid model. "dating" serves to solidify the practices, since 7 out of 10 go through that process prior to getting married?

Existing technology such as digital camera which seems to have been deployed within the framework of **digital cameras** mounted in interior and exterior walls of commercial buildings, is facilitated by the Internet, has numerous applications else where. In reality, it is aimed at so many positive uses yet can be used to cause havoc in our digital world. The threat to use this technology to violate an individual's privacy creates, a danger as a frequently, openly used device. To reflect on activities generated and recorded by the use of digital cameras is something to think about seriously, such as;

video clips getting in the hands of undesirables. Clips that portray experiences that others can relate to seem to attracvideo clips getting in the hands of undesirables.t users' attentions.

People love humour, especially when used as entertainment, there is a steady use of humour shown in video clips of approximately 2 minutes. Digital technology that produces motion as used in drones which hover over buildings delivering packages, an addition to inter-net shopping and delivery is being experimented within the package delivery services.

In other circumstances this object is remotely guided over miles to monitor individuals, such technology could be harnessed and used to produce a form of transportation so replacing one of the automobiles of the average household, since the average household has at least 2 automobiles, much is yet to be done even to get to the drawing board.

It is interesting that all the preceding mentioned, digital devices upgraded concepts are linked to The Internet. Innovators seem to have the vision that the digital technology should not leave behind devices and equipment driven by the old technology, the analogue. They do have their individual or system uses. They can be subjected to upgrad-ing, and attached with digital circuitry so replacing the old conceptual name, so taking on the updated name, "Internet of Things," (IoT). Industry has embraced digital technology with a high level of apprecia-tion that within the next 2 years, approximately 9000 consumers prod-ucts may be on the market categorized as Internet of Things (IoT). Many of these products are rapidly re-invented and have found a place in the digital landscape of Canada and the U.S.A.

Here are a few of these devices, house and commercial thermo-stats, wearable keep fit devices, digital cameras, animal tags. Farming systems designed to monitor elements necessary for healthy growth of crops can be monitored, keeping accurate tracking of; temperature, light and humidity. In the office sensors respond to data collected showing that everyone in the office has left for the day.

So the heat is turned off. Research estimates, suggest that by year 2020, more than 20.8 billion things connected, fit the definition of IoT which will bring an income of $3.8 billion dollars, USA.

An IoT functional, digital system usually has web-enable digital devices with sensors, processors, and communicative equipment which receive data, acts on the data from the environment then transfers the data to desired location. Some of these devices are so smart that they send data that they collect to other devices then act on the data that is received. These devices have potential to interact with other devices without the help of human. Although humans can make intervention like inputting relevant instructions or inspect the collected data.

From the fact that industry has jumped on the bandwagon of change, utilizing these devices, the potential of household products to go digital is enormous. These devices are no way 100 percent efficient. The "hole" that exists in the devices have been exploited by internet hackers, through cyber attacks.

As digital infrastructure is deployed globally, and as household and commercial equipment are built with Wi–Fi capabilities increasing more usage of internet, the cost of the Internet service falls. As high speed internet meets the demand of analogue equipment converted to digital technology, a new connection and communication between the individual and equipment started to take shape. The average analogue equipment uses an on-off- switch to control it and only is controlled on-site where it is installed. In contrast, a Digital circuit used to replace analogue circuits, increased the uses and efficiency of the equipment. For example, the refrigerator of the future can be access from your office, from your vacation site thousands of miles away as well as from the manufacturer's site. Almost anywhere, as along as working, internet is available to be accessed.

Many of the equipment possessing the capability to access related data around them, evaluate the data and will send focused data toother machine, like the thread mill that the individual is working-out on.

Take for example, that an individual is driving to a meeting, on his way there is an accident that blocks off the route that he is supposed to take to the meeting.

The automobile, equipped with sensors picks up the location of the accident and picks up an alternative route for the motorist. Since the new route taken generates loss-time, the software of the automobile sends instructions to the printer, specifically to print information for the meeting suggesting that road blockage has created loss time, in effect will be late by 15 minutes.

As capability of devices and equipment of the emerging technology improves and as sensitive element as decision making is place in the data base of equipment and devises, a new level of interaction, and connection have generated. When it comes to machines to make decision and to think of the possible consequences of those decisions, careful thinking and research have to be in place. Especially, when putting responsibility within the control of machine, is something of interest. The possibility of connecting "Internet of Things" to one another and the "Internet of Things" to individuals via the internet, using the mobile phone, lap top, desk top, the tablet and other devices is a wonderful phenomenon.

To realize that your future, refrigerator has the capability to collect related information from the user, sends it to the keep-fit machine that the user is working-out on, pointing out the poor eating habits of the user, and in turn sends the same data to the thread mill which in turn sends that data to the wearable, wrist band keep-fit monitor all with the intension to improve the health conditions of the user.

Such is the fascination the digital technology seems to have created that window to encouraging self-managed lifestyle with colourful, active visual imagery. As digital technology embraces artificial intelligence in devices and equipment to offer fascination and builds solid foundation that has application in our Western world as well as having global application.

Cyber attacks occur when someone accesses another user's data base with the intent to cause disruption or steal information. Many cyber attackers operate from foreign countries, sometimes whose country do not get along with the country intended to be attacked so making it difficult to bring the attacker to justice. To break in a local citi-zen, computer server, the hacker uses a software referred to as ransom ware and sends it to the email address of the unsuspected user. When the unsuspected user opens this email the ransom ware file attaches itself to the user's server, encrypts the user's files and locks files making the system in-operable.

The hacker uses a variety of strategies, among them causing disruption in the smooth functioning of files that run program files smoothly. Cyber, attackers could even send an email to the user demanding a certain amount of money to be paid before access to computer again is resumed.

It is important to examine the basics of a functional Internet. In the early stage of the Internet messages were sent to home through telephone lines. When the user is Online a telephone message that comes in would cause disruption. At present, Online signals travel via invisible airwaves. At the user's home or workplace, an Internet provider is selected who sends a technician that sets-up a ***modem***.

MODEM & WI-FI

A modem functions like a receiver, whose basic functions is to receiver Internet signals, distributes the signal to various devices in your house or the workplace that feeds from the modem. It is a part of the process as the user is engaged using a digital device to send out data on the Internet as near as the distance between you and the person in the same room and as far as thousands of miles away, globally. The medium that carries and sends out Internet signals, that medium is called WIFI. Television receives television signal and converts these signals into audio and visual imagery, modem receives imagery sends the imagery sends the imageries to our devices which could be, laptop computer, the desk top computer, mobile phone, tablet, iPod etc.

FUNCTIONING DEVICES

Manufacturers consistently are upgrading their software for digital devices so the device or devices used is essential that it/they are functioning well to receive and convert these signals to the desired purpose of the user. Technician sets up your WI-FI and test-runs your device before he passes over the control to the customer.

SOFTWARE AND YOUR INTERNET ADDRESS

Most Internet providers are of a local, venture, so chances are, you are using one of locally organized providers. A part of the deal to use their monthly service, they will assign to you, the customer, an ***Internet Address, commonly called Email Address.*** This address can be a combination of words and numbers that emails, through which other forms of digital information is sent to you.

Your Internet address is very much private. The lock for your Internet address is your password which can be a combination of letters and numbers. One of the main uses of the email address for most users is to send emails. Email is digital replacement of hand written letters. As emails are sent to friends in the form of a letter or note, is also used in the process of buying products Online, contacting firms when doing business, within your emails you may create files that you can file-way for future use.

WEBSITES

Websites offer access to information globally. To access such information the user must be connected to the Internet. This process is relatively simple. Once the user is Online, he needs to type in the website access information. With this piece of information you cannot make any error in spelling, for access will be denied.

A phenomenon of the Internet is that you can stay in the comfort of your home and access information thousands of miles away that someone has set-up that has information you may need. The phenomenon of accessing data thousands of miles away and can get an immediate response is a part of the signature of the Digital Era. When you access the page of your Internet address, by typing in the web page address you are likely ready to access a variety of digital information sent to you, varying from emails, advertisements, documents, reminders etc. Such information is stored in your in-box.

A great bulk of information is accessible via websites. These are; access to information of libraries; universities, health issues, Do It Your Self Projects, Online academic courses, banking, you name it, chances are it is available Online. You can search for information by typing related names or phrases as well as of specific name of the other sites.

Cyber Scammers

It is quite a phenomenon that a user can stay in his/her house and access systems, in another country and makes changes that significantly creates negative effects to the systems, as well as to others connected to those specific systems. Scammers are the spoilers of the Internet. They exploit the gullible, prey on trusting folks, steals the life savings worth millions of dollars of those who often have an honest mind. They disrupt systems such as water, electrical that run cities. Big Data base of firms are broken into and personal information of clientele is stolen. It is reported that rogue countries have hacked into banks and stole million of dollars.

As the Internet evolves there is evidence that power is associated with it. Power in the hands of those who want to use it for the general good for everyone, is usually welcome. But alternately there those who are aligned with scammers that cause much havoc to computer systems of another country. Steals millions of dollars from private accounts, access citizens personal information from data base of private firms only to use such personal information against these private citizens or the business firms focused on.

Ownership of valued resources and distribution of other resources that affect wealth impacts the disparity of these countries and create names such as Third World, and Developing countries which suggest the plight in which inhabitants of these countries exist. These people are people without a lot of things. Among them is, "a voice". Facebook CEO suggests that his social media firm, Facebook, is committed to offer the voiceless individual a voice. This may be a significant move to uplift mankind, especially when access to a personal account of Facebook is relatively cheap.

As Christopher Columbus, the pioneer, declared to curious explorers who were discussing exploration, pointed out that his voyages to the Western world suggested that he had shown others the "way" to exploration. In today's digital era, others may view CEO'S of Amazon and Facebook as digital pioneers that deploy digital ventures or making business decisions that will function as digital business models for others in the future.

If it is our personal desire to succeed and function well in the community that we exist in, maybe we have a moral responsibility to help others to function well in their communities as well. Especially those who have access to enough needed resources. As the digital era brings global communities closer via the Internet, we may discover that there are more commonalities that we share than what we do not share.

Perhaps we may recognize that the continued existence of mankind may depend on participation or contributions from a global perspective. For example,if the general health of global communities are upgraded then the benefits will significantly impact everyone, for the world is just a community next door accessible in minutes. Given the assumption that the individual has the propensity to do good than doing bad, then Digital Technology could just be another media available to factor in the improvement of these communities. The devastating pandemic, Covid-19 demonstrates that we are closely linked than we really realized.

Since there are few firms in our industrial and commercial econ-omy responding to the need of digital deployment to help the infrastructure of well needed developing countries. This could be the hope that the implementing of digital infrastructure is the beginning of overall development. In modern times to be aware that 1.5 million kids of the region of Congo, Africa will die of preventable diseases, it is alarming that such deaths have no meaning to leaders of 7 greatest economy although those leaders seem to have their focus on global development.

There is hope though, as contractors are already installing equipment and materials that will improve the digital infrastructure in some communities in Africa. Communication is available and improved functioning, is evident, as natives have regular uses of their mobile phones. Full uses of email, texting, tweets and the use of some Social Media platforms.

Oprah Winfrey exemplified in financially support, a school for girls in a needy area of Africa. Bill Gates, the big name of Microsoft influencer, and innovator is well known for making financial contributions in areas of needs globally. These are the digital forerunners who seem to function with a national conscience intended to improve the quality of life for others.

As business players take the effort to improve the digital infra-structure, support system and guided direction for the benefit of residents of the various communities are essential for the continuity of this infrastructure. Direction and guidance are needed from these business players. The United Nations Organization which seems to have an eye on whatever is taking place globally, has global goals[5] by partnering with UN the goals could function as resourceful starting point to examine community responses and level of reception to identify community needs. For example, the rush to embrace digital technology in the lives and daily activities of people in developing countries may drive enthusiastic innovators and contractors to seek out initiatives, to execute such initiatives.

Yet such initiatives may not be a top biological and household needs. An analysis of community basic needs such; as Education, Health, Transportation, Water System may be necessary to forge a rela-tionship with community members to see what level of access and use residents are at. To enlist men/women of conscience coming from churches, organizations experienced in charities. Innovators and banking from these communities could be helpful as sources of related information needed to create supportive continuation of related events necessary, for organizational existence.

The digital revolution along with computer technology has made an impact and has been embraced globally, like no other event in the world. Globally, commercial, and agricultural communities have embraced the technology with opened arms. As countries make their move to take their share of the digital pie, country like China expands its digital markers, in Africa. China, although in Africa for sometime, it's signature had very little visibility in the digital restructuring industry but now digital markers of China are surely becoming noticeable.

---

[5] NGlobal Goals a collection of 17 goals formulated by UN assembly in 2015 to improve the quality of life globally; https//www.globalgoals.org life globally ; htt//www.globalgoals.org

CHAPTER 8

A Nation of People with New Digital Profile

A **portion of our daily activities** consists of reactive stimuli that drive us to react, the digital industry provides much stimuli to generate reactive responses. This reactive responses sampling is evidenced in normal behavior in daily activities. In the morning we react by being prepared for the place of employment by waking up a certain time slot. There are certain activities that are performed in preparation for departure to work. Formats are put in place to generate desired responses to prevent chaos from occurring. Institutions of our society function to prevent chaos. Chaos generates dysfunction, creates loss-time, loss time impact the general objective of most institutions.

The emerging, digital technology along with the Internet offers to the individual to move into the Reactive/Proactive Mode. This mode of response is facilitated by the use of digital devices such as; laptop computer, mobile phone, tablet, wearable keep fit devices, digital thermostats, sensors and artificial Intelligence systems and others. Digital technology generates numerous, new ideas which are converted into new products and services. Unfortunately, when new ideas are converted to services and products, some viewed these new products or services as disturbances to the existing an existing operational system intended to be improved. For some of these generate new responses that may not in tune with tradition thinking and tradition behavior.

For as the individual is exposed to the open world, his hidden thoughts and intended actions become accessible. But can he be blamed for his personal thoughts and actions that shaped him into what he is? Since man is a product of his environment, and quite often has no control over forces that shaped his thoughts and actions. Therefore, it is a natural response for anyone, confronted with new ideas, new thoughts, new services to be subjected to a fury of rejections. Although they previously swears that the love everyone an everything and offer 100 percent supportive actions.

But demonstrated wishes to avoid new products and services offered in the digital technology emerging landscape is a phenomenon of personal preference. Since emerging technology has evolved to find its place in all areas of human lifestyle, the buzz phase is, "embrace than escape". Such technology is entrenched in so many areas of our lives, will soon be in areas of preference such as Health Care.

So, devices that bring attention to the user that he needs urgent medical attention are already in daily use. Such devices, alerts the individual that the user needs quick medical attention. The multi-services that the mobile phone offers, in areas which are so significant such as safety, during driving on the public roads, as exemplified is a new dimension in personal lifestyle. The growth and expansion of these platforms indicate the significant purposes they serve. In reality, Social Media may generate disturbance within the tradition thoughts and practices of human responses to social behavior. Since the digital landscape is considered to be undergoing a digital transformation, most revolutions usually bring on disturbances, this suggests that the emerging digital technology has its place on the pages of Revolution.

Two billion plus daily users of Facebook, globally suggest the relevance of the Social Media giants impact on modern man especially those of Western culture. The benefits for the individual are numerous, market makers are surely connected to consumers' networks influencing them to make purchases. It is middle order needs, displayed in social needs at work that yearn for satisfaction. Innovators responses do fill those gaps, in a variety of formats hooked up to the Internet. Social Media platforms have emerged to offer those formats of satisfactions.

The emerging technology has created pathways that lead to activities related to Reactive and Proactive Responses. This is seen in the use of the computer via the Internet to; access, store, to seach for information, to access variety of data with the aid of search engines via the Internet. The average individual store information now, not only in written formats but now in picture and video formats. The process of shooting pictures/video clips and the individual making the decision at what angle the picture/video is shot how many shots are taken, the light on the picture are decisions that the individual has to make.

As the user wears keep fit devices, information is gathered about the user's fitness-level. Devices send data to a site/s that the user can access, this allows the individual to maximize the benefits, which could mean increasing his time on the favourite, health activity like doing a number of laps in the swimming pool or the number of "push-ups" to improve the level of fitness.

In a democratic society, an element of democracy, is the option to make choices. Democracy provides to the citizenry that existing oppor-tunities that necessitate choices. When there are no optional choices, then the individual is almost challenged in a monopolistic situation. The option of choice is dead. The individual is reacting to the com-mands of situations that drive him into that responsive mode. At the early start of the Internet, most users have only 1 option to get on the internet.

That option was the use of the desktop computer. Now, in our digital emerging, landscape, there are several options to access the internet . When there are several choices within the optional framework for consumers, it is generally believed that people as consumers are set to earn greater benefits than when there is no option. This mode is referred to as the Reactive/Proactive mode. Consumers react to such responses by examining the number accessible optional choices.

The emerging Digital Technology facilitates reactive/proactive responses of citizens. Numerous search engines offer the opportunity to search for consumer food products. Easy and quick information access is a new way of doing things. Searching for clothing, electronics, place to live such as apartment, condominium, or town house; related information can be accessed via search engines and other essential utilities is conduct with speed and ease.

When it comes to purchasing consumers items, many consumers[6] usually select the lower pricing if the expected value meets the expectation of the purchaser. Those music enthusiasts who missed the "age of the cd/vinyl," when they have option of buying just a single song in contrast to a whole album of songs, digitalization of music brings them that option again. Digital Technology now offers the option of listening to a single song as well as a whole album.

Information is very much associated with digital technology, the digital technology has put in the hands of consumer the digital camera, imbedded in the mobile phone has become an innovative device of storing and transferring information to others.

The frequent use of contractors, builders at hardware stores with their digital cameras of their mobile phones taking pictures and sending the images to co-worker on site to verify the product desired to be purchased, offer an uplifting imagery for Digital Technology.

The frequent use of contractors, builders at hardware stores with their digital cameras of their mobile phones taking pictures and send-

---

[6] NGlobal Goals a collection of 17 goals formulated by UN assembly in 2015 to improve the quality of life globally; https//www.globalgoals.org life globally; htt//www.globalgoals.org.

ing the images to co-worker on site to verify the product desired to be purchased, offer an uplifting imagery for Digital Technology.

But digital technology brings to the forefront that recording of information is not only in print form, but also still upholds the concept which suggests that "a picture worth more than a thousand words". As situations exemplified in a road accident involving collision of automobiles, pictures are taken to be given to the forth coming police officer. Even more authentic is the digital camera which records the actual situation "live". All these technologies, are hooked-up to the internet, categorized as the internet of things.

The average mobile phone user now has fallen in love with the digital camera attached to it. Almost any event that is related to a physical gathering of number of humans, the current practice is there is need to take pictures always arise. The practice of pictures being taken by professional photographer, still exists but in a limited way. As powerful, digital camera lens now in the hands of the average mobile phone user can produce picture quality comparable to professional photographer.

For within the framework of choices, the user does not have to take the imagery to a photographic shop to have the volume of pictures processed even if they are not to expected standard. Right in the comfort of the user's living hall, he can decide on what to be processed or not. Plus, most devices with a digital camera, offers a gallery for saving pictures to be retrieved for processing at the desired time.

When market makers begin to think of consumers as having product expectations, that's a silent shift from the business practices of the product-demand economy which is usually left to market makers to influence consumers-thinking in believing that they need the product shoves on the market. As clusters of manufacturers embrace the concept, this may be a start of a trend that consumers are moving towards a new level of Proactive Responses within the consumer's market.

May be, as Digital Technology creates new products, new attitudes, emerged and reinforced, a new attitude that needs to be examined is the concept of "engaging facilitates" the consumer with the options to make proactive responses within the digital changing landscape. It is this form of behavior can be referred to as individual participation physically or mentally in the activity at hand. In this digital age "engaging" seems to be heightened as human interact with one another, especially witnessed on Social Media. Giant, internet providers, those platforms create pathways that illuminate digital footprints.

Such footprints entice the user to follow others. As users, using the mobile phone, to make online connections, going on dates, travelling significant distance to meet someone, befriended online which sometimes ended up in a marriage, presents a new form of lifestyles. Physically involved is referred to as opposed to online Dating.

Online Dating is a created spin-off of Social Media. This interaction is extended to mobilizing supporters of specific issue/s. This is also evident in the issue of "Black Lives Matter" where sympathizers are mobilized to attend demonstration globally. The use of Social Media to motivate sympathizers to travel significant distance to participate in street demonstrations, showing their support of a specific issue.

As you are about to cross the street the eyes see a fast automobile speeding towards you, so alert you that you are faced with danger. Your eyes relay the image to your brain. The brain analyses the danger the imagery poses and instructs the individual to get out of the path by running ahead or turning back. This is engaging for personal benefits. While within the digital technology framework, the use of Artificial Intelligence machine in communication with machine to machine, is being implemented in gathering data within the limitation of a specific area.

Since the objective is to get the artificial intelligence machine to think as humans, the machine is capable to analyse the collected data and also make rational decision focussing on the data at hand.

As variety of technologies emerge and devices and equipment are built to connect these devices and equipment to the internet, the emerging technology landscape begins to take shape in Canada and the USA. Digital infrastructure has sprung up over regions and communities. There is evidence of digital devices that arrest the attention of those who are curious. Devices that fit the concept of survival of the fittest begin to take roots in an authoritative dominance.

The rise of Social Media platforms reinforced by the presence of the Internet, facilitate the need to transfer large quantity of data from location to location with digital precision and speed previously unknown. Clusters of firms working supportively to produce identified and agreed on products or services have sprung up.

If we examine things in nature that take a lifelong existence, a common factor which is noticeable is the "natural orderliness of things which is common to one another". Biological Ecosystems reflect those elements. The co-existence, interaction and interdependence of all members of a Biological Ecosystem are responsible for producing and maintaining a new resources, eg. a new factory. Similarly, as all the stakeholders within a specific Digital Ecosystem, exemplified within the Digital Ecosystems and within Social Media platforms, produce a great amount of data. Data is therefore, emerging as a commodity. As a result, survival of data is enforced as new uses are found for data.

FIGURE 8-2 Data sources used in Industry. Shutterstock infographics.

This is exemplified in the uses of artificial intelligent devices used to monitor an individual medical health, i.e. heart rate, artificial intelligent devices used in gathering and producing data in driverless automobiles as well as machine to machine communication also shows that data is gathered and sent to one another. With the production of great quantity of data, business has recognized that data has significant uses.

Whether personal data gathered, focused on a specific objective, or for general purposes, the importance data gathered will make a significant impact on the changing digital landscape. Of course focused use such as; an individual health or keep-fit activity, to be used to run a firm efficiently, to predict the purchasing attitudes of customers, or for manufacturing products or services to attract customers. The use of data to customized customers products of specific demographics to rein in those targeted customers, digital technology offers significant uses for data and offers an efficient way of gathering reliable information. Variety of software are available to analyse data to predict high accuracy outcomes. The use is so widespread that during 2016 Presidential Election, in USA, analysed data was used to examine how some demographics responses would be used predict responses to certain civic activities.

CHAPTER 9

The Digital Ecosystem Foundation for Digital Products and Services

Digitial Ecosystem embraces the concept that implies that the ecosystem possesses all the resources needed to create a product/ service from the initial stage of the product/service to the selling of the product/service. This system is modelled after the natu-ral Ecosystem which exists in natural conditions. Natural Ecosystem suggests that living things are sustained on earth because these living things exist in a community of supported resources. Similarly, Digital Ecosystems exist to offer all the resources, manpower, skill needed to produce the specific product and market it to the consumer.

Identifying essential elements of both systems reveal their common elements as explained in the following infographics. Since the biological ecosystem exits to perpetuate the continuity of living organism on earth, so innovators, scientists and engineers rationalized and view the emerging Digital Technological industry as consisting of numerous digital ecosystems that possess elements to sustain the digital industry. Therefore, the existence of the concept of "*Digital Ecosystems*".

Life begins in habitats of the ***Biological Ecosystems***, for example birds' habitats are their nests, the habitat of fish is pond or stream etc, the habitat of human is his/her home. Elements that are necessary for the survival of the living things are; water, air, soil, and other living things. Living things usually go through growth-stages prior to maturity. Similarly, the location of the firm is like a habitat, where ideas germinate, nurtured, analysed, and turned into products and services. These are production stages and the final product or service ready for the market is parallel to the stage of maturity. Each stage is more of a nurturing stage, getting the product or service ready to another stage.

The biological ***community*** consists of several habitats, and the interdependency and the interaction of living things with one another is more evident. A community could consist of numerous varieties of living things over thousands of acres. Trees in the communities could provide berries as food for the birds, in the branches of the tree's birds build their nest. While a stream could provide habitat and a living place for a variety of fish and aquatic insecs, these habitants could also function as food for a variety of fish and other aquatic residents.

The digital model suggests that communities are represented by numbers of stakeholders who are connected to firms with their own objectives but make business contributions to the creation of final product or service ready for consumers' use. Also in the mix are research departments of a firm, analytics firms that provide data that suggests what kind of product individuals of those communities needed.

An independent company that specializes in analysing data could make its contribution by boosting the efficiency of the production line by analysing data of robotics connected to the production line. In this way, malfunction areas would be detected, and solutions would be deployed so minimizing breaking-down disruption during manufacturing processes.

Areas such as manufacturing department plays an intricate role in physically, putting the product together, while specialized, independent firms make and supply specialized parts crucial to the completion of the product. As part of system working together, is an independent firm responsibility to functioning as an agency to advertise the product and bringing the finished product ready to be purchased by the consumers.

Within the Biological Ecosystems living things go through a life cycle. In the initial stage whether it is a seed in germination or a baby bird, just hatched, *resources* are needed to facilitate full development to maturity. In the Biological Ecosystems, these conditions are food, care, and protection. Our vibrant digital technological economy has *resources* in place to create new products and services as identified with the rise of social networks such as Facebook, Twitter, Instagram just name a few. Facebook has a daily user of more than 2 billion. In major cities of USA and Canada there is a solid Digital Technology infra-structure that guarantees the innovator access to skill workers, research personnel, market personnel, financial support system, consumers and others. Elements needed from the beginning of the product through manufacturing and the selling of the product. An important digital device within the Digital Ecosystem is the mobile phone as a single device that connects with numerous services.

The application of the internet and the Internet providers con-necting all users to one another as well as connecting globally, showing imageries of the world right into your living hall. If your culture or mind-set compels you to close your eyes and plug your ears, imagery of distant land sits patiently, awaits, you at website, for you to peek at or examine at a comfortable stage of your life.

So elements within Digital Ecosystem are necessary to encourage the springing up of firms to produce and sustain products and services are; a network of firms with updated digital technology, financial investors, government agencies with committed objectives to work along-side the developer of the products or services, innovator/s, company workers and consumers working supportively, and in variety of different ways to create products and services.

One of the interesting Digital Innovative Technologies that has made an impact on the Digital Ecosystem is the use of Artificial Intelligence. Artificial Intelligence used in experimenting with machine to think like humans will have a significant role in human history in the future.

The concept of "Internet of Things" which facilitate most household appliances and other equipment only accessible at home/ or at the specific venue many of these equipment have the capability to be attached with digital connection. So facilitating them to be conected Online.

The effect is that this equipment can be accessed distance away from home, is likely to generate much attention from household users. Also depending on when security is functioning effectively as a part of the whole system. For the equipment possesses useful analysed, reliable data needed for use in making shopping decisions, safety decisions or even child rearing decision. As the equipment possesses the capability to communicate with other machines, is a remarkable phenomenon as great abundance of data will be produced, and ownership of such data may become an issue.

The use of data analysis which is a function of Artificial Analysis in several areas of industry, to generate efficiency of running firms as well as to manufacture products for consumers is another use of Artificial Intelligence having significant implication in the future. But one of the fascinating, projected events that will generate economic activities, such event is the "Internet of Things". Prediction is made that for the next future years more than 10,000 household appliances could be attached with digital connectivity, so allowing them to be connected to the Internet. They have data base to pick up information within their personal space and relay the data to other machines. With a Digital Ecosystems having the infrastructure to convert old analogue systems to digital system, USA and Canada will appear as if the countries have evolved into another planet.

As the year of 2019 draws to a close, evidence shows that the U.S.A has over 6 million jobs positions unfilled. While Canada has 5.6 % unemployment. According to economics standard that percentage falls in the column of full employment and is considered the lowest dating back to 1976. Statistic Canada[7] released information indicating that goods-producing sectors added 26,900 while construction added 14,800, 26,000 jobs came from the professional, technical and scientific sectors, the services added 67,200 jobs. Digital innovation, no doubt has played its part in the growth of Western economy.

Sad to say the disruption caused by the pandemic, Coronavirus by the fall of 2020, such successes were all dashed to the ground. Projection shows though, that as soon as a vaccine is discovered to control that virus, because digital technology with all the variety of deployed technology, such strong foundation will give rise to a strong economy again. Survey shows that as emerging Digital Ecosystems spring-up so producing new ***services and products, there is a degree of urgency to enforce*** proper digital connectivity with the new devices or equipment and already on the market.

Efficient connection will reduce hackers' tactics of breaking in the systems to create havocs. Quality of connection is essential as evidenced in prevention of cyber disruption, especially when systems are inter-connected. It is noticeable that devices produced by specific firms, the connection between them is functioning on a relatively efficient level than with those not produced by the same firm.

The efficiency of connectivity cannot be overly emphasized as it is an area of point of entry , cyber pirates use to break into devises to disrupt the order of things. or service initiatives, intended to increase likely, to increase efficiency.

---

[7] Labor Force Survey Statistic Canada, December 2018 htt//www.statcan.

This is exemplified as analysed data used business objectives. Among new products that capture their interest is the driverless car.

These automobiles are built with sensors and actuators[8] working together, placed in digital circuitry, along the roadsides where these cars are being tested to function to collect data and send such data as required to control station.

For example, in the experimental driverless car, the driver's in the experimental process, is faced with his automobile systems subjected to make decision in seconds. Factors involved are accurate analysis by on-board computer system and speedy transmission are necessary to avoid an accident. While manufactures of automobiles uses data col-lect by sensors to predict the reliability of the automobile when driven under certain road or weather condition suggests a high level of per-formance expectation. Digital Ecosystems with automobiles driving on the street without a driver is likely to reset the mind are; super com-puters deployed in the driverless car to initiate quick decision. Sensors installs along the roadway from which the driverless car pulls data to guides it along the journey. The application of self-driving will likely has trial use in many areas as has begun in delivery of consumers prod-uct to storage locations.

Using analysed data, at a high level of accuracy, focussing on con-sumers' products can be tailored to fit the purchasing needs of consum-ers. When consumers data is collected by machines and transfer-red to another machine, there is indication that effective management of such data needs close attention.

There are many questions that need to be answered. Will that kind of data create a pathway of its own? Or is it needed to be channeled to a desired route?

---

[8]   An actuator is an electronic device that responds to computer signals. It is used with computer to turn off devices or digital systems.

Predators of a biological ecosystem disrupt living things within those systems. Similarly, cyber pirates, and hackers functions within the Digital Ecosystems, cause disruption.

FIGURE 8-1 Functional operation of Cyber Security to keep out digital predators of Digital Ecosystems. Shutterstock infographics

While in Canada, pattern of disruption done by cyber pirates seem to take a different pattern. Noticeably, was that cyber pirates were chiefly focused on large data. In the year 2017, study shows by Global Fraud Index[9] that in USA $3.3billion were lost by mer-chants accounts were accessed by internet piracy, while in $57.8 billion accounts for cyber fraud.

While in Canada, pattern of disruption done by cyber pirates seem to take a different pattern. Noticeably, was that cyber pirates were chiefly focused on large data. Interestingly though, when they get access, "Big Data," a usual technique is to utilize their access like criminals by using a pattern of coordination in their activities.

When they purchase items, this pattern presents itself. They retrieve data in small volume, to prevent suspicion. Even activities such as unusual, monetary spending in purchasing goods signal to security expert to investigate a possible connection with cyber pirates. The use of algorithms is used to detect, Fraudulent money movements

9 Global Fraud index REPORTS/Signifyd, September2017.com

spending pattern eventually revealing the link with fraudulent activities.

Bear in mind that strategies used are focused on not being caught. The industry though fight-back with the use of Artificial Intelligence machine which has the capabilities to detect patterns within the systems that suggest an attempt of piracy. Consistent patterns show that one of their objectives is to stay hidden, while security objective functions is to catch the pirate.

It is disheartening that when one is caught and put out of business, there emerges another, just like a biological predator which has a place in the biological ecosystem, the cyber pirates and disrupters seem to have a permanent place too. But as we embrace the natural order of things and create systems to protect elements of Digital Ecosystems will innovators eventually deploy systems in place to deter the bad guys out of business by sealing off the various points of Entry. Then in a humanistic approach, show them a path to use their ability in a supportive role in the evolving Digital Ecosystem. If everyone belongs to Digital Ecosystem, then There should be a appropriate place for every resource person in the Digital Ecosystem. Since it is the nature of man to do good instead of bad deeds, then Cyber Pirates as resource persons may just gravitate towards participa-tion in positive contributions[10].

Let's hope that their existence is not partly to fulfill the con-cept that suggests that we do not live in a perfect world. There are some critics who suggest that if frequent changes are made in the user's password to prevent break-in more challenging, that procedure could be a start of finding some reliable solutions.

---

[10]   The Information and Communication Technology Council, (ICTC) suggests that Canadian innovation landscape facilitates a third party.

There are some critics who suggest that if frequent changes are made in the user's password to prevent break-in more challenging, that procedure could be a start of making a strong security statement to cyber pirates. As technology becomes smarter, control and even maximum break-in prevention may be a reality of the future.

As Social Media generates big data, and when data is analysed the potential value is recognized, no wonder cyber pirates recognize that there is much value in data. The Digital Ecosystems in and around the city of Toronto demonstrates that Toronto has become a hub for Artificial Intelligence. Since Artificial Intelligence devices produce a lot of data, and as data is analysed, and as machine sends data to other smart devices, it is noticeable that data is slowly emerging as a signif

cant commodity in Toronto.

The great amount of data being generated and the application of data in so many areas of the business sectors show a growing use in consumer products/services as well as industrial application. A few applications may stimulate thoughts to discover other applications.

Analysed data is used to market products for specific demographics of consumers. The information gathered has been used to monitor mechanical parts of racing cars during the actual race to identify parts that need to be changed so preventing the racing car from breaking down. The procedure suggests mechanical parts that are subjected to much pressure as in the case of industries. Parts under stress are identified and removed to prevent break down to avoid loss time.

As "Big Data" finds itself a comprehensive, market globally, the importance of data urges big players to begin to strategically position themselves to show their dominance, Canada is all set-up for this. Players develop a Digital Ecosystem in *Application and Services* in areas such as, *Health, Commerce, Transport, as well as other areas.*

The rush by so many players to find a habitat in the Digital Ecosystem suggests that digital technology has emerged to find application in numerous areas of existing consumers needs and in the areas of industry. It further suggests that the technology has emerged to a level of readiness to be deployed in numerous areas of need. The "Wildfire" concept is used to explain the numerous activities the technology generates and how the ecosystem accommodates Digital Technology.

A component of the Exchange Theory has become evident and it is that "wildfire component" *that suggests that authentic digital innovation will generate "wild fire effect".* Such an effect is usually a reactive effect as shown when a wildfire starts, there is much enthusiasm to; (a) find the causes of the fire. (b) To alert those that are a threat to the fire. (c) To utilize controlling methods of the fire (d) The grief associated with those burnt out.

Similarly, the technology pulls all sorts of players to react to the application of the new technology, from continued research, product, enthusiasm of consumers/industry attitude towards uses. Users that often create a new cultural image, plus innovators enthusiasm to make a "big pay day" from digital innovative technologies.

There is an exponential effect of the technology as other countries utilize the technology to ensure that they are not left behind in this New Digital Technology Revolution to keep it alive and pushes the digital ecosystems to keep moving from city to city and regions to regions.

This manufacturing model, Digital Ecosystem, embraces a cluster of business, supportive human interaction, relevant manufacturing materials or services, supportive government agencies, reliable high speed Iinternet networks and reliable Internet service providers, working supportively to produce products and services that are in such demand that these products and service have no market boundaries. boundaries. They are products or services of a global demand as well as for global yearning.

This model, although you may find that it is deployed within major cities of the USA and Canada, and has application elsewhere, the sustaining model is also used in Europe, Asia, Africa, Australia and New Zealand, Mid-Eastern Countries, is evident that it has global application.

This Digital Ecosystem model allows the powerful Apple.com head office located in the USA whose employees working on the production of its smart phones in China communicate with Apple workers in USA. The Digital Ecosystem, like the Biological Ecosystems takes us back to our origins, shines the spotlight on the basic elements that nurture life and awakens our minds ,reminding us of basic interactive elements that exist within the Biological Ecosystems that holds life together, and those that foster sustainable interaction.

But as users who are all tarnished with the drive to seek individual preservation, there is much difficulty in embracing the emerging technology. For as those humans who are troubled by their outdated thoughts, which keep reminding them that it is conventional wisdom to reject anything that carries little elements of familiarity, as elements of Discovery, Exploration drive us apart, humans have lost familiarity.

Digital Ecosystems pulls workers together and shatter the isolated personal space by connecting one another as everyone works together for a common objective. Workers recognize that ability is shared in all colors and body shapes. The potential to discover that humans share more commonalities than things that are not common are reveals as humans interact with one another.

May be, the abundance of information brings individuals together, identity is acknowledged, and similarities are discovered, then human nature of similarities that force people together like shared fresh air needed to breathe, clean water to drink those commonalities may evolve or strengthen, one another, reaching out to one another, pulling them together to exist in harmony, the projected Digital Technology harmony, like the support and harmony promised by elements of the Biological Ecosystems.

Much care has to be taken by security personnel to prevent entry into any of the systems that drive the driverless car. No one will predict what strategy cyber pirates will use to solicit some benefits from their break-in, if they have in their control a driverless car system that could be instructed to be a road-traveled missile. Another

The possibility even exists that where preceding world events such as, Discovery, Exploration, Industrial Revolution, did not bring some innovative technology that is positioned to impact the digital landscape . The group of technology, which used to be run by the old analogue system, this group of digital technologyis the "Internet of Things" offers significant readiness for use with new technology.

Biological Ecosystems

•HABITATS
- A place where living things eat, live and reproduce.

- COMMUNITIES
- The existence of resources for the use of members of all who depend on such resources.

- POPULATION
- All the living things that exist and function as some form of resource which could be consumers and producers.

- PREDATORS
- Those that disrupt the cooperative order of things in the habitats.

Digital Ecosystems

•HABITATS
- The manufacturs site to rese product design and manufac finisded product/ service.

- INDUSTRIAL/ COMMERCIAL COMPLEX.
- A venue where those involv work collaboratively to prod the end product.

- POPULATION
- All the human resources tha whose function as workers i production process and thos consumers to purchase the product.

- PREDATORS
- Are indivduals who delibera disrupt the functional syster especially digital systems.

FIGURE 8-2 Common factors that exist between Biological and Digital Ecosystems.

The possibility even exists that where preceding world events such as, Discovery, Exploration, Industrial Revolution, did not bring some communities may get another chance. That chance could be made available by executing the digital Ecosystem model along the Internet of things. Evidence of impact of Digital Ecosystem on technology and jobs have been so evident in Canada fast developing transformational city, Toronto.

So Digital Technology has really been transforming the techno-logical landscape, we know that the Internet has rob us of our privacy, but at the same time has brought global communities to us right in our living hall. As business models function in thriving Digital Ecosystems.

There just could be a message for those who cannot get along. They are reminded that such an interaction, cooperation, and exchange of resources that function at the workplace are evidence that individuals on a broader basis may co-exist starting with identifying commonalities that they share.

The market value of numerous resources in national as well as global economy is amazing as the continuity of these resources is made possible by the existence phenomenon of the Digital Ecosystem.

> Toronto, A Canadian model of a successful Digital Eco-system

The Digital Ecosystem suggests that within digital technology framework, start-ups, ventures and existing business can develop with all the required players working collaboratively to produce products and or services. This is the application of The Digital Exchange Theory in its highest form.

Toronto, the commercial capital of Canada with, its easy going, polite, people have enjoyed the quality of life which is among the best in the world. Toronto is model city of "multiculture" implants where residents co-exist peacefully. Given multicultural landscape that visitors and global writers observe no wonder skilled workers needed for Digital Technology work force are attracted to Toronto. The supportive approached by The Federal Government when processing foreign applicants for work permit in Canada, for the technology industry creates feeling of welcome to these technology workers. The feeling of being needed is evident. Majority of new technology workers enter from the USA, India, China, and Brazil.

In addition, the technology work force does absorb skilled workers from well educated workers graduated from adjacent universities such as; University of Toronto, Waterloo, University, Ryerson and York University. These universities not only have technology programs second to none but have technology labs of industry and of world-class standard.

With the great number of motivated entrepreneurs with high quality education and financial backing, start-ups of world class have sprung-up in various parts of the city of Toronto, as well as Markham, neighboring city of Metro, Toronto.

An area of Digital Technology that Toronto excels in is Artificial Intelligence. Artificial Intelligence functions to get machines to think as humans.

The year 2017 investments in Artificial Intelligence starts-up amount to $191 million. Investors such as BDC, MARS, Inova and Fonds de Solidaire are some of the prominent ventures that make their names in the industry. FTQ is involved in Health Care while Mars Ecosystems focuses on Uber researching driverless automobile. Big names technology firms seem to have their focused-on Toronto. In 2017, Google invested $5 million in the technology lab, Vector Institute located at the University of Toronto. Blackberry, the Canadian trail blazer mobile phone maker, has been focussing on making technology for driverless automobiles. While Samsung, in Toronto has focused on the Artificial Intelligence business, in the area of Health Care.

The establishment of 1.5 million square feet of working space called MARS Discovery District, accommodating more than 100 machine-learning, venture firms is evidence that the Digital Ecosystem in Toronto is real. Among the Artificial Intelligence ventures that will impact the North American market, domestic as well as the global market; is the Uber Artificial Intelligence venture. It is involve in researching, driverless cars, while there is Borealis Artificial Intelligence which focuses on Artificial Intelligence research for the financial institution.

Royal Bank, Borealis focused on state-of-the art machine learning conducted in Toronto and Edmonton, Alberta. Areas of priority are; fundamental and applied research focusing on; (a) Reinforcement

Learning (b) Natural Language (c) Deep and Supervised Learning with the intended focus is to solve ground breaking problems. This lab is state of the art lab headed by a professor of Artificial Intelligence.

Research in Artificial Intelligence is a slow process, scientists and researchers are much aware, so much dedication is expected as well, as workers focused to generate positive results. For as analogue equipment goes digital, the learning that each equipment needs, are likely to differ from device to device. Plus, it is not only the task of programming the equipment to think and produces data. There are numerous issues in programming machine to think as humans. But when machine is expected to generate information relating to an individual health in an area which could mean life or death, then the level of accuracy of information puts out is very essential.

The establishment of Borealis Artificial Intelligence suggests that Royal Bank has recognized that within the Digital Ecosystems partnering is a 'buzz' word, so no doubt Borealis is positioning itself to fulfill its needs just like other businesses within that immediate ecosystems. To reinforce the concept of Digital Ecosystems as a long-term entity, Royal Bank is offering scholarships to students intended to enroll in master and doctoral degree-programs in Artificial Intelligence.

As city service delivery personnel, installing analytical cameras in high traffic areas or at areas of concerned, video data is analysed almost in real time generating data to allow the personnel to make instant decision to enhance safety and security. This allowed an attendant to go to the site of concern to fix the problem.

When there is a need to closely monitor issues caused by nature, the use of smart technology has its legitimacy as exemplified in preceding situation. The technology is also deployed in almost similar situation in monitoring a storm water pond.

In Richmond Hill, a city neighboring Toronto, the need to monitor water pond at the pond monitoring station in real time draws the attention to the use of smart technology. As real time data was sent to the operator at the monitoring station, safety for motorists was enhanced as attendants were sent at the identified area on time to enhance security for those affected.

As innovators create a new culture with the driverless, automobile, utilizing smart technology, to bring to the public driverless automobile, so attention is drawn to use of smart technology in monitoring parking tickets meters. Customer's convenience and employee efficiency have been enhanced as parking lot attendants can stay indoors, especially on a cold wintry day and remotely monitor the parking meters. They have the capability to adjust the visible pricing demand i.e., low-traffic time slot is tagged cheaply, while high-traffic time slot is priced the most expensive. Users within access limits, via the use of their smart phone's Apps, process their individual, payment remotely, instead of facing the cold weather, or leaving the warmth that indoors offer on a cold, wintry day.

Digital Ecosystems have been springing up all over North America economy. As they spring up, they impacted the world. The United States has offered leadership in new digital innovation that consumers embrace with opened arms. As this business phenomenon has demonstrated that the interactive and cohesive elements that drive it to produce goods and services for customers will solidify the continuity of new start-ups.

Other countries have created their models as the uniqueness of each country may dictate the successful model. However, among the various countries of the West including Canada especially Toronto, countries of South America and Central. Also applicable countries of Asia and Europe some common elements seem to be evident that motivate the springing-up of these Digital Ecosystems functioning as a base for the manufacturing of digital products and services. This common elements are discussed later.

As digital systems are deployed in industries using robotics, sensors, actuators as well as Artificial Intelligence, there is disruption the normative operation of business. Most ventures may have full digitalization of their business as a long-term objective while for others' objective could be focused on a short term. Whatever the objective focused is, strategic inter-connection between all the operational systems is necessary, to generate a smooth functioning of the deployed systems.

The accelerating in digitalization of industry and smooth transition from analogue to digital suggests the impact of digital technology on changing landscape. The deployment of technology such as the Industrial Internet of Things, Gateways, Interfaces, Entry Security, 3D Printing, sensors and actuators make forceful impacting statement on innovative changes that are occurring in industry . As innovative technology impacts industry to transform it, business is impacted in so many areas that disruption, frustration and other obstacles impact management workers and consumers.

Business Activities: Front-line workers, management, human resource personnel even if they are positioned to cope, will be impacted. As new ways of doing business, become evident, the language that goes with the new systems, and how solutions are used to main smooth functioning of the new systems are part of the new culture that must be understood.

Business Ecosystems: As that specific business become apart of the Digital Ecosystems of the city or region, stakeholders are motivated to work collaboratively in product/services manufacturing and service delivery according to the goals of the firm and the needs of consumers. *A New Business Model*: Digital transformation offers the opportunity to modify the old existing business model. This model whose objective focuses on profit maximization, encourages profits to be locked away in the safe of some of whom are top income earners. This new model would distribute profits more equitably, focusing on those of the middle and lower income-levels. The change could be focused on equitable profit distribution with the hope to increase the living standard of middle class and the lower income- levels.

Human Resources Department: Members of Human Resources often is a part of a team responsible to help employees cope with the new business culture that the deployment of digital systems gener-ates. As the general operations of business is under going changes so are Human Resources employees. Sometimes disruption leads to the deployment of new solutions which in turns caused more dis-ruption which signals that to the industry that disruption is an ongoing issue.

Digital Marketing: Digital marketing creates greater outreach to customers. The accelerated uses of digital marketing via Social Media and big data company such as Amazon and Google impact the ways advertisement is done, now as well as in the future.

Establishing A Changed Management: It is really necessary to establish a focused group of personnel whose members are much aware of the direction in which the digital changes are going. As one of the objectives, is to keep the changes on course. In addition, to offer help to the employees in terms of additional training and guidance if needed.

Customers: As new digital products are placed on the market, and existing products take on new product-features, and filled the needs of consumers as well as solutions for industry. There arises the need for applicable education for customers and vendors. For they are also an important part of the Digital Ecosystem whose roles are important to offer access to information as well as to play that key role to satisfy consumers' demands.

Below are the elements found in Digital Ecosystems that make ventures successful.

> **Common Elements in Most Digi-
> tal Ecosystems**

Innovators: These are the motivated individuals who have new ideas to turn into products or services. They may have the incite of utilizing the already known product or service to be manufactured at another geographically location.

Financing: A new business just starting up needs monetary resources to cover all areas related to producing the final products or services. The innovator may have the capability to initiate fund raisers. The government of the country may designate grants to the new start-up firm. Investors may view the new firm as a potentially money maker, so financiers may be easily attracted to invest his/her personal money in the firm.

Consumers and Market Makers: In most economies, sellers believe that monetary resources used to purchase their products and services come from what is called disposable income. It is the job of, advertisement specialists to influence consumers that they receive the messages delivered to them. The message should be delivered that they understand the message that they really need the products or services.

Infrastructure: Digital infrastructure that accommodates the continuity of business operations is necessary. A reliable Internet to facilitate the moving of data from manufacturers to users. The availability of Internet of things offer potentials to build on.

Supportive Regulation: Governmental support can be in the form of financial aid regulations that protect the new starts-up from academic piracy and the will to "go after" those who are involved in it to compensate the owners of the new start-up. Available Skilled Personnel: Cities such as Toronto, Canada, Seattle, and Silicon Valley, USA really enjoy a pool of skilled and resourceful personnel of engineers, scientists, technologists, frontline workers from which to retrieve specialized workers .is so necessary.

Each city is likely to be different, however, this resource is helpful. As ecosystems evolve churning out services and products innovators have recognized that Artificial Intelligence can be harnessed to run systems with a high degree of efficiency, creates in the moment feedback on essential data and even reduces operational costs. The concept that many city managers all over the world are deploying Artificial Intelligence system to run their cities, is an indication of the extent cities are moving towards becoming, Smart Cities.

One of the elements that seems to drive a Smart City, is continuous connection of people with one another and the Internet, the connection of devices with the Internet, the deployment of the kind of infrastructure that facilitate and enables the springing up of digital ecosystems, and the utilization of the Internet of things ventures are part of these new technologies. Also the willingness of operation man-agers to incorporate the emerging technology to create effective service delivery to citizens of that city.

Smart City generates economic growth, when smart technology, Artificial Intelligence, and Internet of Things are used to run city systems such as; Transport Systems, Water Systems, Education Systems, Light Systems of a city, to name a few. Since smart technology is used in many areas of digital industry, it makes much sense to invest in technology that has application now and will have applications in the future Digital Ecosystems meet that criteria.

Canada having voted as the number one country in the world to live, just before the onset of the pandemic, Covid-19, smart technology could help Canada to maintain that standard of living. Available and in use in urban cites is smart technology deployed to monitor office space within a building and will turn off the heat when the building is not in use. Then will turn on the heat again as the technology monitors the office space, on time for the office spaces to warm up on time for the next user/s.

Safety of building is always a concern in urban cities, smart technology has the solution for safety, the digital camera can pick-up the unusual intruder, analyses the behaviour of the intruder, in real time, relays the information to a security guard to investigate the intruder.

High speed internet is essential to facilitate effective functioning of Smart City, as these Information of Things send data online to other devices as well as to websites, reliable and high speed internet is really essential to facilitate quantity and speed needed to process and send data.

Data is important in functioning of Smart City. Most of the devices and equipment that are categorized as the internet of things, produce data. So, data within a Smart City framework is very important. For example, data tells if there is any connection between pollution and Asthma, and so offers significant information to city planners and so plays key roles in determining the use of bicycles along with pedestrian walkways so reducing the flow of automobiles pollution within a specific area. The application of examining data to prevent health issues is enormous.

As city managers move towards linking utility systems with smart technology, residents do have physical access as well as digital connection to these systems. Such connection allows city operators of any smart systems to make connection with residents in real time via town meetings, communication in time of natural disasters, i.e., flooding caused by rainfall.

Open Data is essential in Smart City in development and in operation as Open Data allows residents access to all Open Data, in effect residents may participate in governmental process. This is exemplified as physical meeting space is not large enough to hold residents who need to make input on decision whether the city should participate in allowing the sale of Cannabis in their city.

Although the mayor and the elected members have the responsibilities in making the final decisions, yet it is important for these elected members be aware of the residents thought on such matter. The city has the option of using video conference or telephone conference so allowing residents to listen to Town Hall discussion, participate in opinion vote and then participate in a follow-up if necessary.

Figure 8-3 Just one of the connecting spaces within a Smart City. Microsoft Infographics.

When large number of residents are connected in a Smart City, they use and produce big data. Big data has much use to business, in marketing as decisions relating to product manufacturing, sales of products, efficiency in running firms are pulled from analysing big data.

Smart homes, connected factories, connected buildings. Likely technology deployed to increase consumers experience are; video, IoT, analytics while users experience smart space in variety of venues such as; shops, street security, Library lighting, factories, residents buildings, train stations, government buildings, hospitals, schools, Smart Space is a digital concept that finds its use in a Smart City.

This consists of digital technology and data access to residents made available to user almost any time. Smart Space is likely to be found in areas such as, factories, resident buildings, train stations, government buildings, hospitals, schools. Some legitimate issues that face urban cities, already are addressed by smart city planners. Such issues as; population growth, mobility within the city, i.e., utilizing driverless automobiles, encouraging the use of bicycle, more designing of pedestrian path, energy management and others are well within the scope of Digital Technologies. In addition, use of LED lighting systems for streetlights, such a system proven to be an energy saver. The deployment of these improve the quality of life of residents.

CHAPTER 10

Impacting Digital Culture

FIGURE 10-1 Engaging is impacting visible change in Digital Innovative landscape. Microsoft infographics.

As individuals, we have choices when confronted with change. We may either react instantly, wait and see, or avoid the stimuli. When the stimuli, i.e., Digital Technology is unknown to us, our ability to rationalize what the outcome will be, is kicked in. In the case of digital changing culture, the technological culture is so rapidly changing that that the embracing response is not to wait and see. It is, what can I see now? This is so evident with the Zoomers Generation. Since they are born in heat of Digital Technology, they lead the digital pact with great enthusiasm embracing whatever Digital Technology available in consumer products or deployed in product manufacturing.

The aggressive marketing makers strategies seem to influence consumers attitude to formulate a proactive response by engaging in these products and services instead of adopting a lay-back attitude. Such response parallels the scientific analogy that suggests that every motion generates an equal and opposite reaction. This analogy legitimizes the emerging digital concept of "engaging". It is a new attitude of being involved than relaxing to the thinking of, "wait and see." As individual participation is expected, leaders will have to move among the audience and listen to the pulse of the audience and encourages responses. The Town Hall Meeting's model is a start.

If the change that is desired is limited to mental activity, then the individual can fool himself and others around him that he is making accommodations to respond to the changing technology culture. Digital transformation generates engaging responses, action, discovery, motion, visible representation, cooperation, enthusiasm, and appeal to the moral fibre of the nation.

In this digital age, engaging seems to be encouraged, as humans interact with one another using social platforms. The use of the digital phone camera encourages engaging as personal information in picture or digital formats are recorded for personal use. Engaging is significant in students learning, the concept is encouraged as some school districts encourage their students to bring their digital devices to school. They are encouraged to make use of their devices to access information, to verify information, and to conduct keep track of their daily school activities including homework assignment. Individuals increased their communications as they are engaged in texting and emailing communications.

It is that enthusiasm that humans mid-order needs, the needs to socialize, to be acknowledged etc. give rise to a variety of social media platforms, to offer several links to those who may have been disconnected, to the greater society and so being alone. Where migration and other forces left family members disconnected, not able to afford the high cost of telephone messaging as the urge to communicate with distant family members seized their attention. Digital technology in the form of email, mobile phone and social media platforms offer cheap and instant communication opens the rescue door to the user.

As humans get connected globally, data is produced and shared, through the analysis of data, humans recognized that they shared many similarities than dis-similarities. Data is taking shape as a commodity. In a commercialized culture commodity has value where there is value favourably connection is likely to hooked-up. Personal data creates a part of your digital footprints which can lead others towards you.

Digital footprints are like digital markers that may allow others to get back to the individual who owns them and can be used to access related data of personal identity. An individual personal identity being stolen causes much havoc in that person's life. When it comes to the user of any digital device Online you are open-up to the world. In effect you must protect your personal identity. To do so you use a personal password and software on your computer that prevents intruders to get into your computer system to steal data and to cause havoc. It cannot be overly emphasized that once you are connected to the Internet that privacy door that you formerly enjoy is no longer there and via the networks the world can get to you. As you prevent unwanted access to your computer system, So you must adapt a responsible attitude in accessing information as well as giving out information.

Connection to the Internet allows the user to access more information as never before. You may be surprised that there are others in another part of the world with a name similar to your name. They may not look like you but may have the same name. There is much significant implication to this. So, as we supply our personal data when called upon, it is necessary to take extra precautionary measures. Like, enquiring if the data will be transferred to other sites that the firm owns. Enquire how safe the storage of your data is.

A significant part of Digital Technology that impacts our way of life is communication and our culture has risen effectively to embrace it. *As we react to digital stimuli, be much aware that there are times when history opens a page to us, to make an imprint, do so by having in mind the imagery of the needy not necessarily to be the centre piece of your decision making, but having some thoughts of whatever help can be offered for it is in our nature to care for the less fortunate person.*

Surely the mobile phone is a significant, evidential piece of our digital culture. Many individuals use that phone to wake them up in the morning, to offer signals of reminders of special events, transfer money from one personal account to the other, look for shopping specials in consumers products, and guide them when driving to a new location, to send and respond to instant messaging, i.e., texting.

Texting by the phone and email by computer shut down the long waiting time-span that the formal hand written letters generate and opens easy access to those of the upper level of the authority structure. This new digital culture, email and texting are sharply replacing letter writing and note writing which have been around, for centuries.

So instant engaging is desired instead of sitting back and wait. Engaging is a buzz word of digital transformation as seen in Town Hall Meeting formats. There are variety of Online newspapers and magazines available to send information to you and influence your thoughts. The concept of trending and viral brings much attention to Internet users and social networks users. Where the rich and famous usually be the makers of "trendy" initiatives. Now Digital Technology puts trendy initiatives in the hands of the average individual. Social Media platforms, may claim ownership for the change. When a posting goes viral it suggests that many users' attention has been captured and have viewed the content.

- ***Expectation and attitudes*** are mindset motivations that drives your responses the way you react to the emerging digital culture, be much aware of these two elements as you embrace the emerging culture. Since it is understood that Digital Technology is another form of technology that is destined to revolutionize society significantly as the Industrial Revolution has made its impact on Western culture, so the expectation is that many of the cultural elements will be subjected to changes.

Already experiencing some form of changes, are; email, Social Media platforms, the variety of uses of the mobile phone. Since we live in a society where there are laws that protect our citizens, an expectation is that government lawmakers will enact laws to protect the citizenry from prowlers who roam digital communication media to cause disruption. So, as we embrace the culture, we do it with a measure of caution when it comes to security. But within that framework you will maximize the use of elements that meet your consumer needs as well as other needs.

Suppose you need to maximize your communication with distant relatives or friends as you have been prevented by the high cost of telephone services as in the case when the land phone system was the usual option. Now, the use of Social Media platforms to send your information in written or picture format is just one of the possible options. Social Media platforms offer many opportunities for social needs to be satisfied. In some countries the lack of activities for retirees and seniors may be replaced with activities emerging from Social Media such as membership chat groups, Gifting Groups, Dance Groups and groups that focused on sharing updated information on topics of mutual interest.

Perhaps one of the most digital stimulants that will arouse curiosity is the driverless car. Since individuals already aware that our existing automobile is dearly loved by individuals of Western culture. Given this fact, it is quite likely that the driverless car will be significantly embraced by the average person when it has reached the level as a safe consumer product. For this machine is dearly loved and is so integrated in Western culture that innovators investment in Digital Technology will significantly impact another area of Western culture, specifically the automobile culture.

Artificial Intelligence technology is deployed in automobiles to create the "Driverless Car". To think of a driverless automobile sharing the express way could be an idea of fascination to the rider relaxingly driven in that automobile, while the other driver at the steering wheel controlling his/her automobile, may have an issue of concern. To satisfy such concern or curiosity is to examine the basics used in driving a motor vehicle remotely.

Driverless Automobile Basics

There are 3 Elements basic to the driverless Car.

GPS systems, which pick up roadways and direction any information within the environment of the automobile that will affect the car that may result in an accident.

A detailed mapping systems of Sensors and radars that have the capability to pick-up road conditions that will have some form of effect on the driving process. Examples are high trafficking, detour, flooding, heavy snowfalls.

An Algorithms and Processing System that analyse all the data received and suggest the best possible outcome. If the data analysed consist of data that is not reliable the prediction generated, may not be reliable. Therefore, the importance of generating data that is accurate, as decision making on the road by the

driverless car will be heavily dependent on data gathered and feed to a super computer of this driverless car.

Never-the-less, the prediction was that by 2021 there would be thousands of driverless cars on the highway as well as some will be on the local roads. In numerous cities of Canada and the United states, trial testing is still going on. There have been few alarming accidents in the trial processes. A significant concern is that when the system of the driverless car has to respond to an unexpected or non-traditional behavior of a pedestrian in close proximity. Such situation usually ends into an accident.

- **With the disruption of the Coronavirus specifically the economy along with the numerous challenges that come along with the driverless car, such prediction was not realized .**

- **Driverless Automobile is Expected to Have:**

- **A manual override so if necessary, the driver may take over control of that car in case of emergency.**

- **Is built with an appropriate seat placed in front of the controls for the use of a driver, if necessary.**

- **The person who sits in front of the control should be a licensed driver.**

In our Western culture, people seem to demonstrate a fascination with the automobile. As a matter of fact, the automobile helps to define the lifestyle of the rich and the famous. It is one of the factors that help to define the Western culture. So, if the automobile helps to define Western culture, it is not surprising that innovators have embraced a cultural legend as the instrument to factor in shaping the culture of a nation. It is likely that the driverless automobile, when it is completed.

As the automobile is already a cultural icon, is likely to established itself as a digital icon within the digital landscape.

Although there are technological giants involved in the manufacturing of such cars, efficiency as well as affordability are hurdles that manufacturers have to overcome. As the digital stimuli that the driverless car triggers, so does a degree of concern is triggered off by other drivers who share the roadway with the driverless car.

To realize that an automobile traveling at a speed that could define it as a deadly missile, being controlled by computers and you as a motorist, driving just meters away could be just frightening. Manufacturers of the driverless cars are likely to share those concerns. May be that is why the use of sensors, radars and cameras, high efficiency components, are deployed to map out the environment of the automobile as it moves from one environment to the other. What road hazards that are beside, in front of, or at the rear of the automobile, are picked up by high quality sensors and such information is feed into powerful computers that analyse the data and best, possible responses for the benefit of the driverless car, and others within its immediate environment is suggested.

Before the driverless car may start out for its destination, the automobile is equipped with ranger finder sensors and high efficiency cameras to detect objects of interests within the environment. This is the route that will lead to the destination. Ranger finder sensors have limitation, from 100 meters to 200 meters. So close attention is placed upon what the objects are and distance each object is, away from the driverless car.

Issues such as safety of pedestrians have come up as essential concerns. May be allowance has to be made for the pedestrian not functioning safely, like not obeying the road traffic lights and so places himself/herself in danger of the driverless automobile as well as and other, objects around the driverless cars. The deployment of high quality cameras, focused on taking pictures of roads traffic lights, road signs and pedestrians are added security.

Recording devices such as special cameras are attached on strategic areas of the driverless car. Identified areas such as; front grill of the car, on the rear windshield, on the side-mirrors are the main points. These cameras pick-up data from strategic areas of the road the auto-mobiles have traveled on. Focusing on areas such as; markings that separate lanes, speed alert signs, vehicles with high beam lights, as well as vehicles following relatively close.

As data is picked-up fast efficient central computer, analyses the data. The passenger/driver will be alerted if there could be a possible accident and the time span to act to prevent an accident. For any reason, the driver does not respond within the analysed time frame, the radar system along with the central computer is designed to take over the braking and steering controls to prevent an accident.

This is artificial intelligence at work at its highest level. It is predicted that at the most efficient level the responses of the computer driven machines are likely to be more efficient than responses of humans.

Ultrasonic Sensors are efficient sensors used to give specific data as to how far away the vehicle in question is away from the driverless car. These sensors use high frequency, so high that the human hearing cannot detect the sound waves. Such sensors, the long range ultra sonic also have application in driving the auto pilot systems.

Wheel speed censors record the speed of the wheels and then sends such data to the automobile safety, systems. Some work along with the navigation systems of the car light based radars, known as **Lidars.** They have significant applications of creating a high quality 3-D profile imagery of the target-object. The high resistance to varied weather conditions, solidified the future uses in this digital marvel, the driverless car.

As these high-quality sensors and cameras pulled in data from the environment, the driverless car, as it goes towards its destination, all of this data is fed to the central computer, the data is analysed offering the best possible outcome for the driverless car and its driver as well as for the users of the road and the surrounding environments.

Driverless systems used in these automobiles are based upon what engineers refer to as ***Deep Learning*** and Artificial Intelligence. As sensors and cameras of the driverless car gather data from the environment, analyse the data and suggest possible, rational decisions. The probability for errors to occur during the process is there, relatively low. Despite records shown that accidents have occurred, such error is likely to be eliminated in the future.

For these sensors and camera supply data to be analysed, the reli-ability of the data is essential. Although manufacturers and innovators are expected to use technology of the highest level of efficiency. Unavoidably, some form of interference is likely to creep into the data so affecting the accuracy of that data, therefore affecting an essential purpose of the trip like directions and suggested responses.

In the USA and Canada, there is an average of 2 automobiles to every household. In some cases, in a family of 4, everyone owns an automobile. So it is quite evident that the automobile is very popular in the culture of Western culture but is the average household ready to embrace the soon to be new automotive culture, driverless car?

Innovators will have a big task with comparative pricing, since a high-quality sensor experiment within the driverless industry could cost as much as $80.000 USA, already more than the price of an average car. Technology usually, free-up time allowing those involved to use the available time to do other things. This may just be so, as applied to the driverless car.

Upon the highest level of efficiency of the driverless, car the user may feel so comfortable that he/she may just want to do a part of his work as he/she is self-driven to work. ***But be aware that technology appears to be perfect, can shift to a mode of imperfection, with negative consequences. So, the need to be on the alert is always important, than just relaxing.*** The one-to-one ratio perception of automobile ownership may significantly change, as the automobile may function as a family shuttle vehicle instead of personal ownership. Just dropping off and picking up family members according to preferential needs may just be a new shift in perception and practice.

Parking lots may be viewed in different ways for instead of parking in a parking lot for the whole day the automobile could be directed to return home to the owner's personal driveway to park for the rest of the day. The sensors of camera mounted over the driveway could send a signal to you, via your smart phone or computer at work that the automobile has arrived. You could open the door from your workplace to let the car in the garage as the security number of cameras are part of the Internet of Things all hooked up to the Internet.

As cars to household are decreased issues such as pollution and vehicle congestion are like to be impacted. The less vehicles there are on the road, the better it is for the city.

Driverless cars may seem to generate fascination, but at the same time elicit curiosity along with concern for safety. So, the suggestion is that care and caution are taken into consideration. To ensure reliability and confidence in people that will move within the environment that such vehicle moves about, 6 levels of autonomy are designed for the driverless car.

From levels 0-2 the expectation is that the driver is in in controlled of the driving and sits at the controls of car. While at levels 3 to 5 it is the opposite, the vehicle is in controlled, and is expected to react to issues and take control of the driving. Research shows that currently, most self-driving automobiles on the road are at the level 0-2.

At the initial level, level 0-2, the automobile system has no independent control of the vehicle but can alert the driver by issuing warnings. At the highest level the automated systems of the automobile take charge of running the car, reacting to messages sent by sensors, actuators, super computers. So, what it is digitally that have crept in the Western culture that has transformed that sector of the culture? As we think of the Western culture as an affluent culture, the expectation of the impact is more towards an improved quality of life. Then surely, an area that has significant impact on digital culture is the Internet.

The Internet has connected individuals to numerous networks reminds us that humans are destined to be connected to one another than being separated. Fast movement of data is associated with Digital Technology, and boosts communication globally.

The average person has the need to utilize the services offered by data in picture and written formats.

As existing analogue technology as well as new Digital Technology come on the market and are hooked up to the market, the growth potential of that market is amazing. When users of analogue devices see their familiar consumer analogue product now being driven by a new technology, that must be an easy way of guiding consumers and the larger market to the supplier/ manufacturer especially if those consumers have product-loyalty commitment.

It is the supportive nature of the Internet gives rise to Social Media which supports the operation of Websites which facilitate access to platforms. as multi-service ever expanding global indus-try. Internet transferring of data at a fast speed.

The Internet is basic to the origin and emerging operations of new Smart Cities, and the use of city-systems to create smart homes in a lifestyles where, the applications of smart devices are used abundantly help to strengthen this application.

The fast movement of data offers to big business as well as small business, access to global markets so encouraging market competition. Without the Internet the experiments conducted to market the product driverless car, would not be possible.

The federal Governments of USA and Canada have realized, the importance for community members to have access to high-speed Internet. To this end, in 2018 the Canadian Federal Government has 'ear marked' $500.00 million Canadian dollars for digital innovation including Internet access. When Federal governments of developed countries have recognized that any cultural element has become personal right, then such an element is engrained in the national, identity of the country.

This is a step forward by the Federal Government to shine the search light and remind all that we in the West have recognized the importance of the technology.

As changes impact so many areas of the Western culture, the changes hopefully, do not eliminate those values handed down to us way beyond the Industrial Revolution. As the possibility to embrace a new business model, referred to earlier, where the element of "profit maximization" is modified to take in a small piece of "profit distribution" could be a discussion by "special formed work groups," and business organizations. Distribution of profits would significantly serve to help, especially those of the middle-income level as well as those at the lower income level.

What may seem as solidly fixed and is untouchable, in time of constant changes, may open to rational examination to generate a rational outcome. As innovative technology encourages, "engaging concept," in contrast to passiveness, citizens have begun to shift from the bondage of passiveness to the freedom of being engaged in thoughts and actions. So, the average individual involves in engaging activities seems to have emerged with a supporting element.

(a) Suppliers of; Labour, (b) Consumers of products but also as an emerging a third component (c) Engaging for self and general good of all. So, empowering the powerless and opening the voice of the voiceless. As he is engaged, data is created these basic proactive engaging elements are likely to facilitate engaging activities as people mixed with others, exchange ideas and service and learn of their varied needs and issues that impact one another.

Digital technology motivates individuals to be engaging. Engaging could simply consist of activities such as work groups involving in planning, within a committee, taking collective ideas to management of their organization to be examined. As well as an individual recognize that he/she has ideas that a community needs so he/she creates a podcast to transfer that information to them. Some organizations have begun the engaging process by accepting and examining ideas that reflect the collective idea of all or most, participants can relate to. The conduct of a simple survey of the organization or work-groups to obtain everyone's opinion on issues important to the venture could be seen as an act of input in the organization. It is could be a surprise that you have significant commercial value as you have several thousands of followers.

As Generation X, graduate from high school, college, universities they come to the changing workplace and other venues with a cultural mindset of participation and digital imagery of change, they will make demands to actively participate than merely being listeners. To walk beside leaders with their "brands" seeking attention, even to take a different route to get to a common, agreed goal. For the old Industrial Era responsible for shaping many thoughts filled with outdated ideas has started to give way to digital Era which is like a wildfire, "*drawing much attention to action.*" This attention to action is a rarely existing opportunity of embracing the ripple effect of change generated by Digital Innovation culture.

That ripple effect of change has weakened the wall placed around established systems, inherited practices show signs of forced readiness to open-up and ready to embrace changes necessitated by technology.

Customs are good but we have to be aware that they do not only carry the writings of those who create and revel in the outcome that they generate. There are those who already in charged with the skills and the mantle of authority to enforce the act of expectation. Especially, if the custom generates a wildfire effect, so empowering the powerless, giving voice to the voiceless, inserting into the mix, a culture of mixed practices.

Education like other areas of culture has been impacted by change. Formerly, access to information required for university and college courses were only available at university libraries and on cam-pus courses. To get to these sites, require time-consuming traveling, now many university libraries are Online, and materials are accessible to the public by going Online.

Entrepreneurs have converted the mobile phone into the magic wand of the 21st century. A user could be talking to someone on another continent, thousands of miles away and within seconds is using that same phone to ordering dinner for the evening at a restaurant in the user's neighborhood. Not sure of the direction to get to a store to pick-up an item, no problem. The information is accessed and becomes visible in the form of a road map or instruction can be available along-side the map with voice instructions.

As the user awaits the delivery of dinner, he realizes that the fire alarm sensor is beeping without any indication of real fire. So, on the Internet, he searches websites on the topic of, "How to fix a beeping fire alarm sensor. Within less than 5 minutes the user finds a,"How To" site that explains the basic steps the layman can use to remove a beeping sensor, cleans it and replaces it safely. Before the user goes to bed, he remembers that he needs to print the 2 tickets, he had ordered for the weekend performance at the theatre. The user is not finished for the night, for as he searches for the website of the theatre, he is confronted with an advertisement referring to a holiday vacation in the summer, as for future use, he has marked the vacation for the nearby future use. In the transforming landscape this is the practice of Boomers, Millenniums and of course Generation Zoomers.

As humans connect and interact socially with other humans, the need to interact grows greatly, so emerged the social network platforms. The social aspect of Social Media is important and has significant impact on culture. It is very important that language has been impacted by the emerging digital technology for those who have been educated to understand there is a significant difference between spoken language and written language in reference to the English Language, they may understand the place in communication in reference to the emerging of "texting". So now kids of the digital culture will have to understand the place of spoken English, Written English and Texting.

School curriculum will have to be modified, to teach the relevance of texting during the processes of communication. For an element of digital culture is doing things speedily, texting embraces speedy communication. So, to embrace that element of the digital culture, it is natural that same data may be communicated in less quantity of words, as exemplified in two letters are used to replace a word of 4 letters, eg. 'ur' is used in texting instead of the word "your". While in texting many users may capitalize the word 'UNHAPPY' in the middle of a sentence. Such use may have applications in the process of "tweeting", but standard writing rejects such usage in formal writing.

People like to express their right to exercise their freedom of speech, under personal names or pseudonyms. Social Media offers welcoming practices as exemplified in Facebook, Instagram, Twitter, WhatsApp, and LinkedIn. But the danger faces the communication, is that Social Media platforms are still emerging and as it emerges there is lack of standard. Politicians use Twitter as a format to call attention to policy comments of various governmental levels. The 45th president of U.S.A uses Twitter to communicate his feeling on anything that impacts him as the U.S.A, President.

Educators remind their students that in establishing an argument, "consistency" is important, consistency is an element of logics. Tweets as well as spoken words by individuals in leadership roles seem to discard the concept of consistency. The concept of absolute truth seems to be dying. ***Absolute truth has universal legitimacy. It has no replacement, not even by*** leadership roles positioned to cast limitation on it. The use of "alternate truth" as a replacement has no origin or continuity but functions to cover inconsistency in the argument at hand.

Never-the-less, as Digital Technology continues to offer communication access that to the average person, the citizenry must be aware that prior to the existence of such communicative platforms only the selected few has access to express information to the public. As the communication formats of Social Media evolves, the long-term benefits will be for the general good of the people. For gone are the days when leaders fight to control their followers by application of "Command and Control Leadership Styles". Leaders may not quickly embrace Social Media formats right away. But Social Media may just be the begin what educators have recognized and encouraged, that better results are obtained when students are engaged.

Organizations and institutions may use guided strategies to generate responses in keeping with the values of their organizations or institutions. As individuals we do have an identity, so are other people of the world. I am sure that you may be able to think of some of the features that identify us with others of other parts of the globe.

Think of some of the digital technology features that identify us with other users. We use digital communication in our everyday communication, namely; email, texting for formal and informal communication. Through the use of the Internet, we have become Internet savvy enough to access information from web sites, located at other side of the continent. Since the technology is always improving, mainly for higher efficiency, the need to be aware of changes is necessary.

Emails revolutionized written communication. In our Western culture it takes a letter to get to the destination within the city and its immediate surroundings approximately 3 working days. The contrast with an email, that from the time the user clicks on the send button, in a matter of minutes the email is delivered anywhere globally, (as long as the digital infrastructure is functioning to standard) the contents of the email is accessible. An important feature of "email is the speed it travels and is delivered to the recipient, in comparison to letter/note written and delivery systems.

For the individual user at home, the user needs to purchase an Online service that creates links to the Internet. Your service provider will let you choose your own email address. This is your digital house address that allows friends and business to send you digital information via email or even commercial messages that fit your communicating habits. If you have a Social Media account, related information may even come to you via your email.

You may recall that the Internet has destroyed your privacy entrance door. So as this Internet highway comes into your home, for now, via your email, you can prevent intruders by (a) blocking the entrance with your private personal, password. Since there are intruders who have mastered the arts of breaking in others computer system, or tablets, service providers recommend the use of virus preventative software to prevent intruders, commonly called hackers from getting into your computer systems. To get on to the Internet the user must have the service of what is commonly referred to as Wi-Fi. Wi-Fi is a shortened name for Wireless Fidelity, the shortened name is commonly used.

Depending on your computer you may have a built-in transmitter that receives this signal or a plug-in adapter ready to receive the signal to connect the device to the Internet. Wi-Fi, as it is comes encased in the form of a box plugged in the wall ready to transmit signals that the desk top computer, the laptop computer, the tablet and the smart phone, also those categorized as the Internet of Things and other devices need to receive and so connect to the Internet.

The technician who represents your Internet provider will install your Wi-Fi box and helps you get onto the Internet. Because the signal is wireless, it is not limited to the confinement of your home or restaurant, other users could access your paid Wi-Fi service and increase your monthly bill. To prevent that you will use a password and a user name of your own creation.

Email requires of you that you need to access it at least once each day. If your work involves the use of email in communicating with employees and clients, then it is essential that you access your email according to the suggestions of your **administrations**. The format for writing an email is very much like a letter, The email-address of the person to whom you are sending the email to must be 100% accurate or the email will not be sent. The body of the email is very much like a letter, depending if it is formal information or social/casual.

The email is so set-up to prevent error in transmission when the recipient address is already in the system. In that way, you the sender do not have to type in email's address. A click on a specific button will do it. Plus, you can set-up an address book that keeps track of most of the emails that you have received. Picture and documents can be sent as additional information on the format refers to as attachments.

Contents of your email that you have received and sent can be treated as information that can be filed away. This means that you can create folders for different subjects, then drag and store each email to the specific file that you have created. If you are not skilled in this area your support confidant may be able to guide you. Your Gen. Zoomer support person is likely to offer a helping hand if needed. Or the pooling ideas of Millennial user, the Boomer user and the Gen. Zoomer could form a cohesive conversation piece for the family, so creating a family chat centre-piece.

To send an email you have to be familiar with a word processing software. Most computer and tablets come with a word processing software. From the fact that such software is user friendly, makes the email processing to be relatively easy.

The use of software offers almost limitless boundaries. Word processing allows you to type short messages or long messages, short stories, write a research paper, create flyers used to advertise an item you want to sell, write a play using a play format. Word processing allows the user to upgrade the presentation of his message, making your finished product looks like it just comes from the printer in terms of quality.

Business is a sector that the Internet has significantly impacted, it facilitates business to collaborate with players needed to function supportively with one another to deliver the main objective, goods or services. Maybe innovators, engineers, technologists, creators support workers and consumers as each functions as desired, as a part of digital ecosystems, so embraces and ensuring the continuance of business model driven by Digital Technology. As a result, the concept of the business model, needed to drive digitalization globally, so Digital Ecosystem is endorsed.

CHAPTER 11

The Internet of Things
Predicting The Future

FIGURE 11-1 A variety of digital devices and equipment connected, to the Internet, commonly referred to as the Internet of Things (IoT). Shutterstock infographics

The **predictable comfort and uses** that device within the emerging digital landscape offer us, is much embraced by consumers. These devices such as smart phones, desktop and laptop computers and our tablets offer us, the users, the possibility to create much reliability and acceptance of services. Steadily, emerging in great numbers within the household, are devices that are connected to the Internet. These devices have amazing capabilities to change the lifestyle of humans. How humans interact with digital devices, the use of data in impacting decision making is astounding.

As we embrace the impacting technology we have begun to live within a digital infrastructure, where equipment systems and devices compel us to make decisions that affect us. It is noticeable, emerging in great numbers of household devices that are connected to the Internet which have amazing capabilities have begun to change the lifestyle of the citizenry. How humans interact with digital devices, the use of data in impacting decision making is astounding.

These decisions are not repetitive, vague decisions, but rational decisions comparable to any rational person equipt with the specialized learning for the specific situation. For devices carry artificial intelligence systems that have high level intelligence cable to make rational and reliable decisions. Such decision will require the individual to respond to such decision physically. But in the business industry and elsewhere, changes take place. Sometimes the visibility of the change, appears to secretly hidden under the blanket within that affluent society. As the expectation of the citizenry is so high that when technology break-through occurs to the level short of a miracle. Manufacturers of commercial and consumer products have wowed us with these products. Central to these, is the Internet of Things

In the early part of 2019, The World Economic Forum suggests that by the year 2020 the number of digital devices that are connected to the Internet are likely to be 50 billion devices. The fascinating implication is that as these devices using artificial intelligence systems offer the possibility to communicate with other devices in the home. In effect, devices deployed with the capability to respond to the variety of data that each device within the environment, sends out or receives, is amazingly facilitated by the Internet. Very much at work here is Artificial Intelligence systems, giving instructions to other devices, generating desired responses to facilitate certain activities until the homeowner gets home from wherever that homeowner is coming from.

Already is a possible function, the user distance away from home, accessing these devices, as turning up the temperature in the home, monitoring the security systems, that is checking if any intruder's picture has been picked up by the monitoring cameras while in the future. Communicating and doing things virtually are timely creating a slot within the digital landscape. During the Covid pandemic technicians of television signal provider facilitate repairs of problem signals by conducting remote repairs from the firm's control center many miles away. Individuals with technology having the capability to initiate activities at locations distance away suggests significant implications. As you move about with your mobile phone it has the capability to record your activities for the day. There are numerous devices that will soon be connected to the Internet, becomming a collector of data. Such data has commercial value.

Data stored in the refrigerator could request the refrigerator to scan all the storage food stacked in the kitchen to establish the quantity of grocery remains in the kitchen. Base upon shopping habits, the fridge would make a grocery list, then, forward it to you on your smart phone for you to pick-up grocery on your way home from work. How is this possible? The use of Artificial Intelligence systems that gather information from specific area of your home, or from specific devices or from you the resident, computer systems analyse the data and make rational decisions.

Since Internet of Things will be creating data responding to data send by other devices. You will be a friend or enemy of the machine which can capture your data and sends it to your account or to others for example your gym director who monitors your keep-fit program. As the keep-fit machine retains data on your keep-fit program it communicates to you informing you of your level of fitness. Because all of these devices are connected to the Internet you can communicate with them via your smart phone. You can even monitor your home from work.. You can do so if you install a face recognition camera which identifies faces of those that come within its environment. Although you may not be at home you may even monitor whoever your kid is taking home as he/she is returning from school. The camera can be programmed to alert you if it captures an unfamiliar face entering your home. Sounds like science fiction, the possibilities are even greater. As 5G technology is developed and deployed in Western culture, global application of this technology is not limited to generate hours of dinner table and business lunch discussion. It is positioned to impact the technology landscape, reshaping culture as never been witnessed, since the Industrial Revolution.

As effective, connectivity among devices, become feasible, manufacturers market devices in packaging. Devices, such as security camera, door sensors, window sensors and alarm system sensors are sold in packaging. Since all devices are usually manufactured by the same firm, connectivity between the devices is usually functioning at a relatively high level.

If a burglar attempts to break in the house by the door, the sensor at the door will send a signal to the alarm system, as well as to the sensor attached by the window that a " breaking in" is in progress, the smart sensor of the window recognizes that the act is an act of ill will, so sends a signal to the smart phone of the home owner alerting him that there is an intruder, the message is that greater efficiency is reached when manufactured devices and household appliances function as a team, the result is usually positive. The concept of "Smart Cities" are not limited to Western culture, for experimental purposes, Smart Cities have been created in Dubai, India, London, England, including cities.

But civil rights pressure groups tend to see a downside in gathering data that Smart Cities produced. The downside is focused on the way conducting surveillance on people is done. It impinges on residents' civil liberties and privacy, they claim. They claim that vulnerable groups such as; immigrants, and demonstrators, such data can be used against them. Their argument gets legitimacy when a face recognition firm made advancement to sell face recognition data to the local police force of the city being surveyed.

In numerous areas of business, workers along with supportive groups seem to generate the outcry that workers will lose their jobs to robots. But the reality of what is occurring is that administration seem to understand that robots are placed in jobs that are repetitive and have high turn-over. Many employees seem to welcome the use of robots in this position, for the placement robots free-up these workers to enable them to function in positions that offer greater gratification.

According to the Council of Economic Advisers, USA in 2018 the research shows that large numbers of jobs done by workers, offer little satisfaction to those employed in those jobs. As a result, staff retention in those jobs is problem. Robots could be delegated to do those specific jobs, so freeing the workers to function in higher order job satisfaction. This is evidenced in mechanically difficult jobs; robots help to get rid of stress associated jobs linked to mechanically difficult jobs that let the worker feel uncomfortable during the working process.

There is the trend to mass-individualized products in the future, meaning that consumers expect that products should be tailored towards their needs instead of consumers adapting towards the use of these products, while in mass production of products in the industry, 3-D printing is making an impact in the industry. With the emerging use of 3-D printing technology used in automobile parts which always be in demand, can be manufactured to precision of the original product. This is done using a 3-D printer whose function is to print the product. This is another indication of digital technology being deployed in the digital technology industry.

The concept of a firm collaborating with other firms to work together, to complete a final product or service is not new in the business world but when business has adapted that model as the model that will ensure the continuity of the digital industry says much of the cultural impact digital technology is having on culture.

The use of simulation in industry, predicts efficiency and allows technologists to see what things will be like, prior to executing the real project. This process has been a significant upward development for the digital culture within the business sector. Whether a new product is being tested as part of the Assembly Line process, or to justify the efficiency of a consumer product prior to delivery to the market, or examination from start to finish of a whole manufacturing process, simulation allows a close-up examination of product-design and a look at the end-product prior to completion.

In this way, future mal-functioning within the systems is likely to be detected and corrections be made to the process or equipment which-ever is applicable. In this way, preventing loss time and identifying and control essential component weakness so moving towards a more efficient product delivery timeline.

As digital machinery produces data in the industry there will arise the issues of managing data. Most factories usually consist of multiple departments designed to enhance efficient and smooth production purposes. It is quite likely that data from one department is inter-related. So, the need to prioritize the objective use of data, as within such accumulation lies valuable information for the firm. Continuous examination of related data from the production department, for predictive, purposes according to objectives, which could be regular maintenance of production machinery, setting pricing in sales department. Or even lowering energy consumption within the firm. As many IoT devices and equipment systems hooked up Online, remote 'trouble-shooting' will increase. During the pandemic many firms try their hands on doing remote repairs. This process involves the customer at the other end as an active, participant, often is not an easy task. But as process is in the incubation stage, this process is going no where.

This is the work of Artificial Intelligence at work. Data and more data, as these machines are designed to be more responsive as humans will the data created reflects decisions that workers made?

Could such data be used as an element in the evaluation process of the worker? Maybe another department may evolve in the firm or data management, independent firms may become a part of the core, as Digital Innovation technology is focused on. As data is outsourced and used in a big way in various departments of the firms, the implication is that analysed data used in relevant departments of the firm can increase the efficiency of applicable departments and therefore the potential for application through the firm.

Security is usually high on the priority list of the firm. The installation of cameras to pick-up data and relay analysed data in real time to the security personnel may just be the starting point for active use of managing data and has significant implication for the future for many firms.

Research shows that 62% of larger firms are utilizing equipment with Artificial Intelligence in 2018. Digital innovative technology has impacted culture and specifically, has begun to transformed Industry that it is digitally trending within industry for manufacturers to move towards digitalization of departments. As firms move towards complete digitalization of all departments, the hope is that within the near future full digitalization will be achieved. When that success point is achieved, that is referred to as, *Industry 4.0 or otherwise known as The 4th Industrial Revolution. We would have left behind* the 3rd Industrial Revolution.

The 1st Industrial Revolution began about 1760 – 1840. Where emphasis was made on deploying water power and steam to replace manpower in factories. The 2nd Industrial Revolution began about 1870 -1914. Integrating within industry were the railways, telegraphs, and electricity. The 3rd Industrial Revolution began about the 1970's, where emphasis is placed on electricity.

The 3rd Industrial Revolution began about the 1970's where emphasis is placed upon the use of computers tech-nology industry deployed in various manufacturing settings.

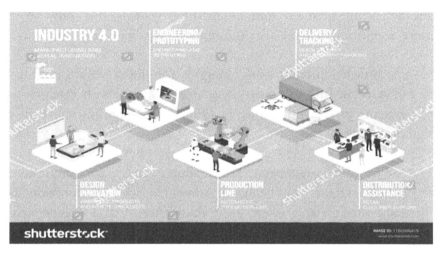

FIGURE 11-2 Industry 4.0 all systems are interconnected, machine runs the industry. There will be very little space for human.

In the fourth Industrial Revolution, innovators predict that machine runs all systems in factories. All systems are connected to one another and are also connected to the Internet.

Steadily, emerging, great numbers of household devices that are connected to the Internet which have amazing capabilities have begun to change the lifestyle of humans, how humans interact with digital devices, the use of data in impacting decision making is astounding. Where humans usually make decisions that affect the activities of equipment and devise, we have begun to live in a digital infrastructure where equipment and devices make decisions that affect humans. As these impacting devices or services influence our thoughts and behav-iors we respond positively to the changes, mostly because we love the technology and we love how the technology plays into defining us as an individual of the Digital Era.

So here is emerging, the 4th Industrial Revolution, intended to change the industry and likely to spill over to all sectors of the nation. Basic to the deployment of technology, is digital technology functioning with interconnecting, functional systems and essential elements, already being used in various existing systems but now at a more sophisticated level are; Automation, Big Data, and Analytics.

At present, humans work alongside computers within industry, to run systems. In 4.0 Industry, machine will work with machine to run systems in the 4.0 Industry . Quite likely robotics will play a significant role in this.

Production systems, information and communication technology systems are being experimented with to function as interconnected systems where great abundance of data is generated. This abundance of data is analysed and used to influence accurate functioning of systems within the firm. Because connected machines are hooked up to one another, communication is expected to flow smoothly between machine to machine. As these machines produce large amount of data, intelligent machine, driven by circuitry known as Artificial Intelligence, has the capability to analyse production-related data. Suppose the analysed data indicates that there is a fault in production line-systems, then that fault can be identified and fixed so preventing unnecessary 'down-time'.

Automation is significant in 4.0 Industry in a small city in Canada, Kitchener, automated robots referred to as self-driving vehicles, like carriers are built to carry within the confinement of factory small weights of 100 kg and 1500 kg. Because data produced is analysed in real time, efficiency within the industry is improved. For example, a ship cargo nearing its destination may communicate with the warehouse indicating the capacity of cargo that requires storage space. The automated warehouse could repack, so creating adequate spacing. As systems are interconnected, workers are displaced, so unemployment may increase. But similarly, in the 1980's it was greatly discussed that computers would replace humans in many employment disciplines, it never happened.

Economists understand the inter-relationship between manufacturers, workers and consumers. They are much aware that workers are also consumers. For consumers to buy products that manufacturers make and sell each need to have a job, this is specifically applicable to the middle-class income earners. Therefore, either the model of machine to machine driving systems have to be changed, to include humans as a part of the team or a modified model to assimilate humans who are likely to be displaced according to that model.

Just like the preceding Industrial Revolution, all areas of society are affected. Already the automated car, also known as the driverless car, is subjected to experiments in numerous cites. It is likely to take on very well, especially as the design of seating arrangements signals a friendly driving trip for a family going on a trip, even a short one. The automated drone has significant current and future uses. Its debut in commercial areas used to deliver, packages to consumers offers hope for application in other commercial areas. In military settings, it is used as a war implement tracking enemies and as a weapon to drop bombs.

If the home is a reflection of those who come from it, then the home is an ideal venue that reflects a change in the technology landscape. The average individual perhaps uses the mobile phone at least 6 times approximately to access services within the day. If the individual works in an office setting, he is likely to use an entry digital security card to gain entry to his office. He is likely to utilize digital technology to send emails on behalf of the firm he works for, on the Internet to access sites of clients, to access information, to purchase services or products.

The home that he is returning to after a day at work has begun to take the shape of what innovators have envisioned as Smart Homes. This means that most household equipment and devices are connected to the Internet and that they also produce data of significance.

Remotely he can use his mobile phone to turn on and off these household appliances that are connected to the Internet. Digital camerras set up in the house allow the user to monitor the kids as they safely come home within the doors of the home. A camera mounted outside on the wall of your house allows the user to monitor the surrounding areas while the artificial intelligence part of the camera analyses any unusual behavior and offers a rational opinion of the situation. Having access to such information allows the individual to act or not. Having access to data offers security and peace of mind.

As manufacturers produce smart devices in packages the quality of digital devices will increase, and so household satisfaction will increase. At home, kids read digital audio books that they download on their computer. Among the source of information for research paper, is gathering data from credible websites. They access homework and other class related information from their digital class sites. The disruption of Coronavirus globally, suggests the need for an Online education at all levels.

While in business, digital communication, provides an alternative to usual work model in place prior to the pandemic.

The quality of student-work presentation is enhanced as each student submit their work for evaluation by having it processed on a word processing software, then have the option of the work print out. There are those who seem to think that when big business invests in a particular industry there is an indication of significant growth in future in this specific area of the industry. So, if this is true then there seems to be significant future in Digital Technology where emphasis is on Smart Homes.

Samsung, electronics giant has launched strategies to develop smart home platforms. As emphasis is placed upon connecting future household equipment systems and others categorized as IoT, predicted to be connected to the Internet as items that forms the smart homes. Samsung has also invested in these areas as well. Google is focusing on smart meters widely used in inner cities, globally.

In Toronto, Canada, consumers seem to embrace digital transformation in various ways but particularly evident are emphasis on the deploying of security and energy control devices. Users may turn up the heat in their homes with the use of the mobile phone at work, one hour before arriving, such decision creates much comfort than arriving at home to a cold house. Residents increased their security needs by installing manufacturers packaging security devices, for doors, win-dows and foyer offer a satisfaction to basic human needs, security.

But the proposal of Smart City at the lake front of Toronto, is an indication that the city digital transformation is at the forefront of development. Sensors are deployed along the roadside transmit information to driverless automobiles on experimental run. Digital parking meters addition to those already in the downtown core of the city offer new options to regulate parking automobiles as well as collect data on how public spaces are used.

As wearable digital devices produce, abundance of data and large open space, in new buildings designed to receive and store data generated by users of this open space, there also evolved the need to manage all that great volume of data. To participate in the efficient management of a special (IoT) data, the mobile phone the 5G technology is introduced. At the initial stage, 5G technology is linked to the use of mobile phone. The emphasis is moving data about 100 times faster than what the current 4G technology offers as well as significant video quality improvement, comparable to high definition, (HD) television.

But there are numerous IoT whose efficiency could be improved, by changing to higher video quality, as well as increased Internet speed. So, application of this technology to improve the quality of the device or the service is a possibility in the future. Major players embrace the concept of Digital Ecosystem. Digital Ecosystem suggests that all elements within the Digital Ecosystem functioned collaboratively for the general good of everyone actively participating in Digital Innovative Technology.

To strengthen digital transformation, not only in Western cul-ture but globally, are technology "heavy weights" that are involved in research and upgrading with the intent to improve the quality of Digital Technology to bring change and fascinations to citizenry using this technology. 5G technology will significantly impact digital culture and lifestyle. ***Digital Technology seems to be positioned to significantly, impact and reshape nations drawing from several innovative technologies.***

Numerous technology "heavy weights" of USA as well as China are participants involved in deploying this technology that transfers data approximately, 100 times faster than the 4G systems, is definitely a game changer in the digital industry. As the stage is set for the appli-cation in the mobile phone systems. So innovators explore the possibility, that this technology could be adapted in the future for consumer's devices, factory equipment systems, home and household devices and appliances, for research and experiment are the usual processes that bring to us these variety of digital technology that we now have access to. They did not happen right away they occur over a period of time span.

Just imagine devices and equipment categorized as Internet of Things, talking to one another, displaying videos of high dimension quality sent at exceptionally fast speed, giving commands, others analysing personal data sent from other devices, even to human who will have to put on his/her "listening hat", listening to devices that add to the existing era of technological sophistication.

Given the demand that the digital industry poses, 5G technology is predicted a necessity to manage all this data producing informa-tion as well as to transferring the information to desired destinations. 5G technology refers ***to as,*** 5th *Generation of Mobile Technology Networks*. Driverless Car is still in the experimental stage, with the use of analysed data to make fast and accurate decisions which could prevent an automobile accident or not. 5G technology has significant place in auto industry as well. The application of high speed technology in driverless automobile, is likely to generate a higher level of efficiency than using 3 or 4G technologies.

Figure 11-3 The driverless automobile creates a new culture in driving, being involved in I or more activities while driving. Shutter Stock images.

Instead of tall tower transmitters as used by current, 2G, 3G, 4G technologies small mini-towers are deployed on buildings to transmit the signals. This technology although has slowly been introduced in some regions the cultural change that is anticipated is so "eye popping" that a technology heavy weight firm has invested 10 billion US dollars to install as part of a foundation of fibre optics, a part of signal transmission systems of the 5G networks. Roadside labs located at bus stops are predictions that will offer consumers, interactive and access to high-definition pictures and videos of the immediate, community facilities. Emphasis is on restaurants, road directions, and numerous forms of entertainment has other applications of this technology.

The facts highlight names of technology giants involved, also demonstrate the technology path and interest that being created at the level of impact of added technological change globally. For as technology giants such as; Qualcomm, Huawei, ZTE (China) Nokia, Cisco, Samsung have satellites plants globally, is an indication the extent in which the technology is impact-ing the digital industry.

Technology devices have many commonalities, each has its own uniqueness. The practice by innovators to apply workable, useful, technology systems in other areas is a common practice. The automobile has numerous systems that makes it so reliable, and this reliability when reflected in the driverless automobile, could have significant applications in other digital systems as in the various areas of 'transportation'. Transportation that has to do with long distance usually caused fatigue. As examplified in train and aeroplane transportations. Like the mobile phone, the potential to apply the technology of the driverless car, for use in so many other areas of transport, is worth looking into.

It may be fascinating to think of yourself being driven by computer systems for an hour or more without a driver, while on the dashboard all kinds of services are flash in your face. Even personal information like the service date reminder of your automobile, is being transmitted to you. Driverless car, although being tested in numerous cities in USA as well as in Canada, and United Kingdom, it is still in the experimental stage. Experiments suggest high possibilities. It is fascinating to imagine going to work, the worker may even view going to work as a relaxing event. As you relax with laptop computer, accessing the work for the day.

Such a phenomenon, of doing some work while on your way to work is not new. But now an extension of what train users going to work have been doing.

As services are identified and prices increased sellers will have to adjust their their services, so as not to price themselves out of the of the market. of some firms seem to encourage digital uses of wearable devices, such as Smart Watch, keep fit devices at minimum cost. Such strategies make the product more accessible to users within that Smart City and so encourages the use of these devices and services.

As devices influence our behaviors, and those behaviors change into cultural conduct, established standards may be impacted, to the extent that the standard is lowered. The user-friendliness of the mobile phone, and various services attached to it allows data to be transferred frequently and far away with very little cost.

So, the issue of value-accepted data that is captured, and the need to display value-accepted behaviour so that data does not come back to haunt the user is significant. In essence, we all become morally responsible for our social conduct in social settings as well as in other settings.

In social settings where data is being captured through digital cameras, mobile picture shooting or video clips are being captured, may be and may not reflect the individual value system. The power of technology to sway behavior and impact change is phenomena of group responses imbedded in the concept of "following the leader". It is for you to evaluate the responses of the leader, in terms of upholding a strong value concept displayed by his/her social conduct. Similarly, you don't have to be a part of the crowd, you may stand up for what you believe in, a stance of personal moral conduct. It must be at the forefront of your thoughts that data transmitted via the Internet to any source, always exist, somewhere in our connected world.

So, the issues of managing personal conduct especially in social setting and being aware of the transmission personal data and how data can affect the individual in the future. Applicants requested to attend job interviews, found out later, that their future employers search social platforms for data that may even reflect negative conduct that might not have revealed at the interview.

The capturing of personal data and transmission or storage has become a part of the culture. Evidence shows that at most social settings, digital cameras of mobile phone users are used to capture data of individuals in form of pictures. Standardize, normative behavior is the desired behavior. There are some who know what acceptable, normative behavior is, while with others the impact of digital technology is so powerful that it could lead to drown out the practice of normative behavior.

So, as not to be caught in situations of embarrassing behaviors, as this behavior could lead to embarrassment later. So, the individual should be very much alert that we now functioning in a digital era where capturing, storing and transmission of personal data in picture format is a part of the digital culture that has emerged to have its permanence.

So, such cultural practices could destroy personal, privacy. Settings such as house parties, birthday parties, held at venues exemplified in restaurants, social gathering at social clubs and sport clubs often considered as private settings. But these closed doors are not safe haven that prevents the transmission networks of the Internet and the gentle activating switch of the digital camera.

As the individual basks in this new emerging culture, he/she should evaluate the environment as he/she enters it. These pointers may be helpful when put in use. Always evaluate any social settings for the deployment of mounted cameras, publicly displayed or hidden. Always assume that participants will take picture during the time slot of your presence. Conduct yourself that a picture of yours will not be a symbol of embarrassment for you.

If your picture is being taken as a group picture or as individual picture find out the specific uses for your pictures. Remember that your picture cannot be taken without your permission.

If you put a drinking glass at your mouth, make sure you know what is in it. Some people lost their acceptable conduct after they had a drink of alcohol. When some people consume more alcohol than they should, their behavior is regrettable. Sometimes others see unusual behavior of others as being funny. If your conduct is being encouraged on, may be its time to take a short "time-out" to reflect on your conduct.

CHAPTER 12

Your Emerging Digital Image

Innovative technology has been so integrated in the lifestyle of work that forces us at the workplace to use some form of digital technology. The use in other areas of our lives has become a normative practice. For example, the use of our mobile phone to access a variety of services has become a cultural practice. Even when we are not at our functional duty, on our breaks we use our mobile phone. The phone has become a part of recreation activities. During the start of 10 to 30 minutes of break from work, more than 50%of us access our mobile phone. At our break from work, weekly events relating to our digital image kicks in. Accessing our friends via social media, for a chat or to get up to date with what is social-trending, to take a personal picture, or to see what postings are on your Facebook, the phone is at use.

The digital generations understand that looking after the body and as well as having relevant information in the data base of the mind are important. With the availability of wearable keep fit devices that monitor the individual's keep-fit level, the weekend is not only for more keep fit exercise but to seek out social entertainment. This involves, selecting, the kind of clothing for social outing, and the right form of entertainment, the digital world offers. High level efficiency is the required path, so selection of the desired entertainment is usually an easy 'act'. A private party-setting, or at a restaurant or just 'hanging out' after "attending a movie" are among the possible choices.

Social Media opens up and brings to users, individuals who will attract the users' attention. It could be body appearance, the kind of music that they like," even the philosophical stance that the personality radiates. For women, body shape is so important ,that as a as a woman steps out of her condominium, in raised high-heeled shoes balancing carefully in her tightly, clad clothes offering a pleasant smile to admires of the opposite sex. If she is waiting for a friend to pick her up, she is on her mobile phone, either texting, making calls or receiving a voice message. If she is walking, she is utilizing her mobile phone, even snapping a picture of herself.

Numerous sessions in the gymnasium shows up the chiseled arms of the male partner picking her up. His tight fitted shirt suggested that he has been "pumping iron" regularly. The focus is getting to a restaurant filled with their friends, all dressed for the digital age. Clothing, hairstyles, shoes, make-up reflecting someone famous, a movie star, a sport personality, a pop star, a model, something, or someone in that restaurant reflective of famous brands or famous individuals. With their devices pointing on the couple entering the restaurant, digital cameras flash at them for the couple is the guest for that evening.

The individual living in cities and regions of Canada and USA, is locked-in a network of Internet webbing, having 3 commercial values to the digital, technology landscape, the firm. They are; the individual as a consumer of digital products and services. The individual as a supplier of labor needed to produce, products or services.

The individual as a supplier of personal data needed to be analysed for business decision-making. The individual is hooked-up to global Internet of networks which allow the world to

access and communicate with him/her, in turn he/she has access to multi-industry of services.

From these 3 elements, digital imagery has emerged in form of digital wearable devices. The mobile phone which has become a cannot-do-without product is a centerpiece of connection. It reflects, new attitudes as seen in the use of social interaction, as users make connection and interact with one another via Social Media platforms. This platform, records and stores picture-data via use of mobile phone camera has become an expected component to be used at any social gathering.

While earbuds or headphone sets in the ears or over the ears suggest that the user is listening to music, privately. Smart City, Smart Home and Smart Automobile, known as Driverless Car, are part of the digital culture facilitated by Big Data and Artificial Intelligence that are shaping the image that individuals have taken. The foundation to devices, digital equipment systems, attitudes and life-styles are the computers, desktop and laptop. A hanging laptop in its casing over the shoulder of the individual, suggests that the user is a post secondary student or professional personnel. While at home there are at least 2 computer-literate persons within the household are reflective of the emerging image.

Digital technology offers several possibilities to recreate a digital imagery distinctly, different from that of the Industrial Revolution. The image may reflect a temporary make-over, where the individual is constantly impacted by consumers products marketed to create a need or consumer preferential items/services imposed upon the consumers who eventually grow into liking the product/s as a cannot-do-without. The foundation of the visual imagery is the desktop, computer or the laptop computer. These devices are presented in the average household. At least one device, or two devices are presented at the average household. Just as the average person is viewed as an educated individual with basic education, similarly, the individual of Western culture is viewed as an individual who is " computer literate".

Although he may not understand the function of the circuitry of a computer but understands how to set-up a personal computer to access the Internet, to connect a printer to print written data or picture data, to connect the device to a television so transfer-ring music videos or entertaining movies. . He/she uses additional digital devices ie tablet or mobile phone to access the Internet. He understands the power of the Internet, so he uses the personal computer to access services such as; Online Banking, purchasing consumer products, get direction within or outside of the city. Partial information for research purposes can be conducted Online are just a few, services that reflect the power of the computer and the agility of the services.

Internet forces the average citizen to be connected with numer-ous networks via the Internet. The average Canadian and American does not leave his home without his/her mobile phone.

It may be a normative practice that the average mobile phone user is expected to access services with the phone at least 2 times each day. This act would make the individual a carrier of least one digital device. It is the mobile phone, the center piece of attachment that largely plays that role allowing the visual imagery of digital connected user.

Like the holster that safely holds the handgun of the old, wild western days, the mobile phone can be attached to a belt around the waist in a leather casing or placed in a pocket of the shirt or dress, in various forms of carrying bags, or just hand-held ready for use, or to make a choice to use it as a "plug-in".

If the user chooses private listening, then the choice of a large headphone set placed over both ears let the user appear as if he/she is in a recording studio. Those who choose the miniature buds, which is plugged in the ear is less noticeable except for the attachment cord from the earphone to the mobile phone. When the user is at home, at work, or on vacation, then access to wireless, miniature speakers allow quality music via a movable speaker box to be taken within a limited space. With the increasing interest in "keep-fit devices" that are wearable and having the capability to send analysed data to the user, the potential for keep fit wearable devices to increase in uses, is a future possibility.

General fitness is not only an important factor in relationship to healthy living. The need to able to monitor significant organs of the body such as heart rate, blood pressure, sugar content of the blood are prioritized areas of the body that demands attention, some people need to monitor on a daily basis. From the fact that wearable, digital vices are available to monitor an individual's blood pressure. The potential to have the digital device monitoring 3 or more organs of the user, offers a permanency wear to the user. There is much potential for arm or wrist band to be a part of the digital imagery. Soon 1 out of 10 may be wearing a wearable device for health purpose.

Wearable, digital devices have started to shape the image of the average individual. This cultural impact can be seen in the form of devices worn on the arm, the wrist, on the feet, on running shoes. Given the option of multiple choice-purchases, our consumerism society adds to our digital identity in digital wearables. These wearables find a place all over our bodies.

Humans are globally connected to numerous networks via the Internet. This connection to the networks brings the individual back to his /her origins to mingle with his/her historical origins via imagery transferred to the living room.

Humans mid-order needs of social interaction are met as the emerging of social platforms evolve to create significant impact on humans' social behavior. The continued interaction forces the adoption of new attitudes towards communication via Social Media platforms.

Laptop computer, designed to be portable offers an uplifting imagery as it hangs from the shoulder of the user coming or going to college, university, or work.

Going to work, the worker may be relaxed with his laptop computer, accessing work as he is driven by a Driverless Car, to his workplace, that is when the driverless car is fully approved to be" road trust-worthy". Currently, using the laptop to access work-assignment in the moving train, while going to work, is a reality, an emerging option, for the trend is that many workers access their laptop on the train as they sit relaxingly. The carrying case, hanging over the shoulder or held supportively in hand is a usual imagery portrayed by individuals on the busy sidewalks of busy technology cities, or dismounting from the parked car, coming or going to work.

Digital technology has carved out a digital imagery in entertainment, publicly as well as privately. The music industry as well as the movies industry are significant areas of impact.

Publicly, it is a known fact that when an individually has an ear-phone plugged in the ear or a headphone clamped over the ears that individual is listening to music or recorded information, being plugged into the smart phone. Most likely it is music.

With the availability of video cameras installed on every mobile phone, you would think that there would be motivation for individuals to take more video clips and even try their hands at creating 3 minutes video clips.

There is the tendency to take more pictures than taking video clips. The use of music videos are evident when individuals are traveling on a long journey. Music video as well as movies on DVD are chosen method for passengers flying for 3, 4, 5 and 7 hours and more.

Home-entertainment, movies available in DVD formats are shown using DVD players or the computers connected to home tv sets or to home-movie sets. As we get comfortable with a product or service, we tend to drop our guards. As the digital waves of technology splash our way we need to embrace the culture with much alertness. For governmental agencies that regulate product and services often are caught between striking a balance between needs of the citizenry and the demanding objective of the business. In essence new technology do have negative spin-offs. This is exemplified in practices of cyber pirates whose objects are mainly to break in user's private, security an disrupt the operational functions of the device's systems.

In the early use of the mobile phones, studies show the negative effects phone signal has on humans when exposed to the transmitted waves over a significant period. Such issue seems to have returned but this time the focus is on the 5G technology. Critics of the highly antic-ipated 5G technology suggest that the form of waves that transmit the signal are likely to be harmful to humans. Most manufacturers of products/and services welcome feedback. Such data usually have practical applications to improve the product.

As people of the West embrace the digital technology, especially endorsed by their governments, history shows that each significant technological impact on culture brings significant improvements in culture and lifestyle. With that in mind, people are expecting that tech-nology will create self-improvement in most areas of existing lifestyles. Especially in areas dear to them, evidence is already seen, in retirement, the use of Social Media makes significant social connections for seniors.

After a hard week of work, people of this affluent society demand some form of entertainment, the cell phone via the Internet have become handy mediums of communication for such events. The Internet and connected devices offer greater scope to access and search for mark-down prices of consumer products to make needed purchases as more choices of access to goods and services are available. The welfare of the future citizens of this culture does look good. As citizens have access to more opportunities managed by national leadership, community leadership and global–cooperative leadership, the quality of life will improve. Such quality will generate a ripple effect having a positive effect on global communities as well. So reinforcing the betterment of 3-dimensioned man, as each continue to offer to this affluent society, Data, Labor and Purchasing Power, to power us into the 4th Industrial Revolution.

Bibliography

1. Bongard, Josh; Kriegman, Blackiston; Levin Michael (2020) Team Builds First Living Robot. Burlington, Vermont University.

2. Couzin, Gradina & Grappone, Jennifer (2015) Putting Reviews to Work. Hoboken, New Jersey, Wiley and Sons.

3. Federal Trade Commission (2016). Computer Security.htt.ps// www.consumer.ftc.gov/articles.1009-computer security

4. Feiler, Jesse (2000) Get Rich with Apps.: Your Guide to Reaching More Customers Making More Money, McGraw Hill, New York.

5. Federal Trade Commission (2016) How to Keep your Personal Information Secure. HTTPs://www.consumer.ftc.gov.articles/0262

6. Federal Trade Commission (2016) Tips for Using Public Wi-Fi Networks. HTTPs.//www.consumer.ftc.gov/articles/0014-tips-using Economics and the Public Purpose public Wi-Fi- networks

7. Federal Trade Commission (2016) Online Tracking. Washington, Dc, Consumer.ftc.gov

8. Gardner, Howard (2007) Five Minds for The Future. 60 Harvard Way, Massachusetts, Harvard Business School Publishing

9. Galbraith, John Kenneth (1956). Economics and the Public Purpose. Park St. Boston, Massachusetts, Harvard Business School Publishing.

10. Keen, Andrew (2015). The Internet is not the Answer. New York, Atlantic Public Press.

11. Lynch , Michael Patrick(2016). The Internet of Things. New York, Liv-eright Publishing Corporation. U.S.A

12. Selkman, Sylvia Silkmen, Benjamin M (1956) Power and Morality in Business Society. West 402nd St. New York.13. Sandler, Corey (2012).Tablets. River Street, Itoboken, New Jersey, U.S.A.

13. Stokes, Abey (2011). Is Thing On: A Computer Handbook for Late Bloomers Technophobes and Screening. New York, Workman Publishing.

14. Statistic Canada (2018). The Daily Labour Force Survey.Ottawa, Htt/www. Stat Can.ge. daily.

15. Thompson, Elizabeth (2019).C.B.C News, November 6, 6.44pm, Fraud-Canada 1.5350865.

16. Torenzano, Richard &Davis, Mark (2011). Digital Assassination: Protecting Your Reputation, Brand or Business Against Online Attacks. 175 Fifth Ave. New York, St. Martin Press.

17. United National Assembly (2015). Global Goals: A Collection of

18. Goals Formulated by U.N Assembly. HTTPs/www. Global goals.org.

19. Vandome, Nick (2016). Apple Computing for Seniors. Holly walk, Warwickshire, United Kingdom. England.

Index of Subjects

Outcomes, market 33

P

Password 6,7,144, 166
Pathway 131
Personal privacy 90,113
Postings 35
Predators 19
Profile, commercial 93
profit 72
portability of mobile phone 20
private account 120
privacy door 99
products 15, 36
practitioners, medical 67

Q

Quality of video clips 67
Quality of life 11
Quick transferring of information 66
Valued resources 121

R

Reactivated information 58
Responses 78
Robotics 192

S

Scammers 10, 86,104
Services15,36
Search engine 3
Security and energy con-
trolled devices 195
Shaping communities 7
Social media 4,5,8,1218,27,30,59,
77, 91,

Software 17,118
Social needs 8
Systems 192
Systems utility 9
Social changes 110
Shaping communities 7
Silicon Valley 109
Stakeholders 83
Starts-up 152
Smart space 160-161

T

Technology, digital 11, 24,
148, 1888-189, 196-197
Technology landscape
3,9,23.91,96,102,155,182
Technology devices 3, 52
Technology culture 51,156
Technology, 5th Generation 59,196-197
Technology, large corporations 198
Texting 13,167
3-Point Model 18, 54,
Transformational, era 73
Twitter 123

U

USA 3, 16, 76
User friendly 19
Unemployment, USA and Canada 148
Universities 152, 178

V

Valued data 58, 86
Videos 56, 59, 108.
Valued resources 121

THE END